LEAD WITH THE RIGHT BRAIN

YDA BOUVIER

Illustrations by
Julie Bouvier and *Rosa Williams*

Illustrations by Julie Bouvier and Rosa Williams

Cover by Stuart Brett, Acorn Creative

Typesetting and publishing by UK Book Publishing
www.ukbookpublishing.com

ISBN: 978-1-3999-4291-1

To my family

Contents

Introduction

'How do you work?'

This is a typical question clients ask at a first meeting. I am an executive coach and my clients are smart, driven, experienced leaders. They test the water with a few coaches before deciding who they want to work with. In a competitive marketplace, where anyone can stick the label 'executive coach' underneath their name, this question matters to their selection process.

'We will be using the right side of your brain', is my reply.

For many of us, our way of living and working is highly skewed towards using the left side of the brain – a consequence of our academic education and the ways in which we communicate and work. This doesn't imply we activate only half of our brain, but rather that the qualities of the left side of the brain dominate our overall functioning. My executive clients (and possibly also you, the reader) are especially capable in such left-brain functioning. It has served them well in their professional lives, allowing them to build strong strategic, problem solving, and goal-achievement track records. And yet, when left-brain functioning gets stuck, it can only be unlocked through bringing in the strengths of the right side of the brain. I am referring to the big, hairy issues that are really important and yet not making enough headway.

For leaders, when it comes to harnessing the value of diversity or inspiring global stakeholders, the right brain is an exceptional ally* (particularly in virtual contexts). In the broader area of building sustainable organizations, the right brain also has a distinctive part to play. On an individual level, the right brain provides guidance through challenging team dynamics, for dealing with stress and pressure, or when navigating career choices. In over fifteen years of executive coaching, I have come to realize that our coaching sessions bring most value to my clients when we strengthen access to their right-brain functioning.

The unique strengths and qualities of our right brain are underexploited, partly because our left brain tends to dismiss right-brain input. Our right brain is able to see the whole, the proverbial wood for the trees, and to see the new, bringing a fresh perspective to situations fraught with complexities and contradictions. Furthermore, the right brain has access to information about ourselves and about others that the left side of our brain doesn't have.

An example of this comes from a recent conversation with Marc, a client, who is describing a challenging situation. He has a lot to share and we are rapidly getting lost in detail.

So I ask him, 'What kind of landscape is this situation like?'.

---

*   Throughout the book, I will refer to the 'right side of the brain' also as the 'right brain', and similarly to the 'left side of the brain' as the 'left brain'.

Marc's immediate reaction, visible on his face, is surprise. I imagine he's thinking, 'what kind of weird question is that?' (which may have also been your reaction when you read it just now).

I probe a bit more, 'I know, strange question, but just out of curiosity – if you were to compare this situation to a landscape, what might it look like?'.

He reflects for a moment and responds, 'It's like I am climbing a vertical rock, with no safety rope'.

We are both silent for a moment. 'What is it like out there?', I ask.

He replies 'It is exciting, I really love the mountains, but it also feels lonely, and I am uncomfortable without the safety rope. That's what is worrying me most about this current situation, I don't feel anyone has my back and I could be left hanging on my own. In my previous role, I didn't feel like this at all.' The rest of our conversation now focuses on his lack of support and how he can build a network of allies in the organization. A key factor in building this network is expanding the support he himself gives to others. In a later conversation, he shares that the original challenging situation had resolved itself once the network started to develop.

As I mentioned earlier, one of the unique strengths of the right brain is the ability to see the whole, without getting lost in detail. In the example above, the right brain provided the visual of Marc scaling the rock which gave us an immediate shared understanding of the situation and allowed us to refocus on the key issue at hand. What is so intriguing is that once we recognize the new perspective offered by our right brain, we cannot un-see it. Sometimes it even seems very obvious; we don't understand anymore why we didn't know this earlier, we might even forget that we once didn't.

The practice of working, coaching and leading with the right brain came to life gradually over the course of my professional journey which led me from Applied Physics to strategy consulting & leadership development at The Boston Consulting Group and then, finally, to starting my own executive coaching business in 2008. Alongside working with my executive clients, I teach executive coaches how to work with the right brain.[1] This approach draws on the learnings from many different fields, including Neurobiology, selected therapeutic interventions such as Gestalt therapy and Family Constellations, System Dynamics, and the best practices of

Leadership development. The foundation for writing this book relies on twenty-five years of experience in work environments. In other words, the approach outlined here is the fruit of a practitioner's perspective, rather than an academic one.

The left and right hemisphere are two entirely different places. You maybe be familiar with the definitions that are often quoted: the 'logical' left hemisphere versus the 'creative' right hemisphere. These simplifications are not fully correct and occasionally misleading, but what is crystal clear is that each hemisphere is unique, separate from the other and, in its own way, essential to us. I am not arguing in favor of using our left brain any less, I am advocating for using our right brain more.

Bringing the qualities of the right brain actively into our day-to-day is not obvious to us because language, our dominant way of communicating, is the processing mode of the left side of our brain. The right side of the brain processes and communicates in images. Hence we often say, 'a picture is worth a thousand words'.

The right brain is also nurtured and activated by in-person interactions. It is deeply connected to our social and emotional life and through that connection we can derive wisdom about ourselves and others.

For example, many leaders have honed their skills to inspire and engage others by complementing words with a powerful physical presence which appeals simultaneously to both our left and our right brains. We are excited to follow when both our hemispheres are aligned. In fact, we really need this coherence between the two. Perhaps you can recall listening to someone and, though what they said sounded logical, you were not convinced without knowing exactly why.

In the age of global business, there is no doubt that executives and professionals will increasingly have to inspire and engage their stakeholders, internally and externally, without being able to rely on their physical presence. Consequently, leaders will require additional skills to fully activate and appeal to their stakeholders' right brains.

The two years of the recent global pandemic, during which we were all forced to work virtually, are another illustration of the importance of the connection between the right brain and our social and emotional lives. A virtual meeting, although often highly efficient and effective, doesn't generate the same sense of belonging, collaboration and sharing. Hours, days, or worse, weeks of meetings on screen can be monotonous, lonely, and draining. In my view, during the lockdowns, we experienced a crash diet for the right brain which severely affected our well-being.

At the time of writing, most of us have returned to our offices at least part-time. Many organizations are asking themselves what the right balance is between office-based and remote working. There are trade-offs between real-estate investments, employee engagement and employee attrition that directly impact profitability. Understanding and learning to activate the right brain when working virtually will help make remote working more fulfilling and, by doing so, contribute to building more sustainable organizations.

But what is perhaps most outstanding about leading with the right brain is that it offers a path to embracing inclusive leadership and making diversity a successful reality. My clients and their organizations wrestle with this challenge. Some of them lead organizations where, despite years of careful investment and good intentions, they are not successful at retaining senior female talent. Others struggle to build high performing executive teams with colleagues from different backgrounds, experiences, or cultures. Some have painfully experienced the many ways in which an organizational system can resist and reject diversity - even if managers and peers, on an individual level, express high support. While we have lived in communities for millennia, our biological make up is such that we are naturally inclusive to those like us, and naturally exclusive to those who are not like us. Our automatic pilot is not inclusive, at least not yet. Appreciating how our right brains connect with each other, paves the way to understanding the simple, practical steps to change this dynamic.

Without doubt, we need the qualities of our left and our right brain to meet the difficult challenges of the 21st century. Yet to use both, we need to be leading with the right brain. Whereas the left brain is a place of 'or' and consequently tends to dismiss the right brain, the right brain is a place of 'and', with the ability to embrace the qualities of both hemispheres.[2] Those who excel at leading with the right brain will be the successful leaders of tomorrow.

This book explores the techniques, tools and practices we need to equip ourselves with in order to access the power of our right brain. This will be done using illustrations from my business experience and coaching practice, underpinned with the relevant neuroscience. My hope is that you will learn that this is easy, immediately actionable, enjoyable and that it has immense benefits.

Chapter One gives an overview of the differences between the left and right sides of the brain. Chapters Two, Three and Four illustrate practical ways to work with the right brain and include many examples. Chapter Five explores the leadership benefits of working with the right brain, particularly focusing on key business challenges of the 21st century – inspiring global stakeholders, diversity and inclusion, and making remote working sustainable.

The following image illustrates this structure. If you are keen to focus on the leadership benefits, read Chapters One and Five first, then dip into the middle chapters to find the tools and practices you are most interested in.

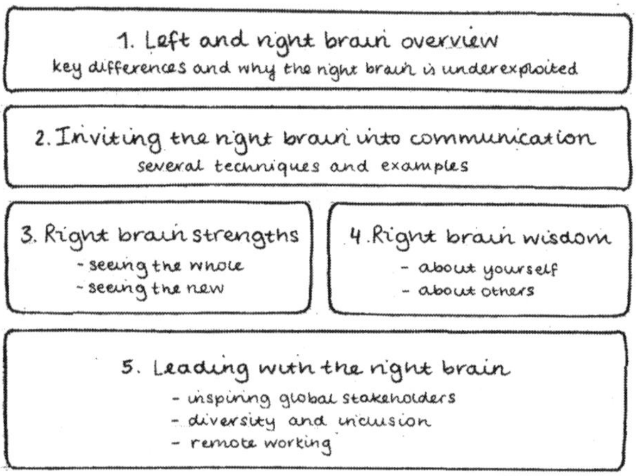

1. Left and right brain overview
key differences and why the right brain is underexploited

2. Inviting the right brain into communication
several techniques and examples

3. Right brain strengths
- seeing the whole
- seeing the new

4. Right brain wisdom
- about yourself
- about others

5. Leading with the right brain
- inspiring global stakeholders
- diversity and inclusion
- remote working

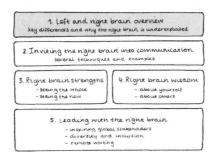

1. Left and right brain overview
key differences and why the right brain is underexploited

2. Inviting the right brain into communication
several techniques and examples

3. Right brain strengths
- seeing the whole
- seeing the new

4. Right brain wisdom
- about yourself
- about others

5. Leading with the right brain
- inspiring global stakeholders
- diversity and inclusion
- remote working

The left and the right sides of the brain, an overview

The image below shows that our brain is divided into two separate sides, referred to as *hemispheres*, which are only connected by a bridge of fibers called the *corpus callosum*. Most things we do activate both the left and right side of the brain, so in that sense there are no left- or right-brain specific functions. Patients with a so-called 'split brain', where the bridge between the hemispheres is damaged, are largely able to function normally, implying that the hemispheres can also function independently. For these reasons, many scientists don't even like using the left / right distinction. So, what makes the left and right brain relevant in our day-to-day lives?

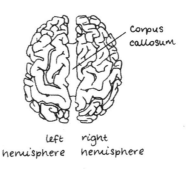

Corpus callosum

left hemisphere   right hemisphere

The essence is that the two hemispheres have a completely different experience of the world around them, and this is what drives their involvement in our day-to-day. A good starting point to see this involvement is in how we communicate, a key driver in how we live, work and relate to each other.

This chapter summarizes key differences between the hemispheres and explores the reasons for the untapped potential of the right brain. To do so, we will dive into the following topics:

- The left and right brain in communication
- The unique strengths of the right brain
- The right brain as a source of wisdom about ourselves and others

Neuroscience continues to develop its understanding of the brain's functioning. A lot of older models about the brain are now considered outdated or wrong, though some still linger in general opinion. One of the earlier theories was that the left brain – known to control the usually preferred right hand – was the dominant and major hemisphere while the right hemisphere was minor and non-dominant[3]. We can take as a premise that the powerful force of evolution ensures the survival of what is necessary. So, as we still have two by-and-large equal parts of our brain, there must be a good reason for both to co-exist. Not only do humans have such a brain structure, but many animals, including birds, also have balanced left and right hemispheres of the brain.

A great deal has been written about the brain in recent years, translating scientific insights into practical implications. For example, you may have come across the distinction between the front of the brain (*Pre-Frontal Cortex* (PFC)) and the back of the brain (*Limbic system*), relevant, amongst other things, to how we respond under stress and pressure. In comparison, there is not much available in popular literature about the reasons and consequences of the clear structural left / right split in our brain. Isn't that curious?

The left and right brain in communication

As previously mentioned, language (in the form of words) is the communication mode of the left brain while the right brain communicates in images. Neurologically, what is more accurate to say is that the motor speech center (the speech engine) is located on the left side of the brain, which is why someone with damage to this part of the brain literally cannot speak. The left and the right sides of the brain can both process language and images, but words are better suited to left-brain functioning whereas the right brain perceives and communicates through visual imagery.

Furthermore, the left brain operates in a way that is sometimes compared to a serial processor: linear, methodical and logical. In contrast, the right brain takes in everything from a single moment simultaneously, functioning more like a parallel processor.[4]

To illustrate this difference, next time you are having dinner with friends, try to capture the experience in words. I tried this during dinner with my husband, and we quickly realized it is near impossible. We could describe what we were eating and what we were discussing, but we could not capture the essence of our experience in words. The experience of our dinner was filled with linkages and connections extending everywhere, how we feel about each other, how the food tastes, our physical condition, our shared and individual memories, our hopes for the evening and beyond, not to mention the weather that particular day. There was far too much going on to capture it all. Yet, if we want to do anything with that experience, besides holding the feeling of it in our memory, we do have to use words. If a friend asks me the next day, 'How was your evening?', I might say, 'I had a wonderful dinner with Laurent, great food and conversation'. She might then say 'Oh, that sounds lovely. What did you eat?'. And I will share that we tried a new delicious Ottolenghi recipe, send her the link via WhatsApp, and she might try it for her next special occasion, hoping to generate some of the same magic.

It is the same for every moment. We try to capture the moment by dividing it into parts, logical and methodical, and in doing so we are able to utilize and share it. This is the unique capability of our left brain, to make the world tangible for us, so we can exert influence and control over it. Still, that representation will always be a simplification, as it was of our dinner.

If I had replied something else to my friend, such as, 'I had a wonderful dinner with Laurent; it was like a trip into our own Narnia', I would have expressed something different about the evening: the magic of the moment, the richness of sensations, and the depth of feeling. The images through which the right brain communicates facilitate this more holistic perspective. I would likely also have had a different conversation with my friend about the evening. Whether I would have ended up sending the Ottolenghi recipe on WhatsApp – impossible to know.

Neither the left nor the right brain interpretation is better or more valuable, but they are fundamentally different and it is this difference which is key to our understanding of how we can use the qualities of the right brain to our advantage.

communicates in
words

like a serial processor ;
methodical, linear,
and logical

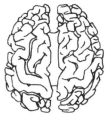

left   right

communicates in
images

like a parallel processor ;
holistic and
simultaneous

When we communicate, we are more likely to represent the world view of the left side of the brain; it is simply the most accessible when we interact with words. It is, in fact, rather ironic to *write* a book on leading with the right brain and attempt a categorization of left- and right-brain differences, but the reality is that this is how we share our thoughts. As such, it is also a good illustration of the magnificent power that language–and the left brain have given us. As so much of our life is impacted by what we talk, read or write about, this reinforces a left-brain-dominated reality.

But there is more to the left-brain dominance. In his outstanding book 'The Master And His Emissary', Iain McGilchrist poses the crucial question 'Why is our brain so clearly and profoundly divided?' After reviewing centuries of medicine, neuroscience, philosophy, history and the arts he states:

> 'My thesis is that for us as human beings, there are two fundamentally opposed realities, two different modes of experience; that each is of ultimate importance in bringing about the recognizable human world; and that their difference is rooted in the bi-hemispheric structure of the brain. It follows that the hemispheres need to co-operate, but I believe they are in fact involved in a sort of power struggle, and that this explains many aspects of contemporary Western culture.'[5]

We all undergo this hemispheric power struggle constantly, and it is easy to notice when you know what to look for. For example: as the right brain doesn't use and control language in the way the left brain does, it doesn't express its ideas as clearly and concisely. We can quickly experience skepticism, or even ridicule, from our rational left side about right brain contribution and consequently, we all too easily dismiss it.

Imagine a business meeting, where a decision is about to be taken, and one of the executives says 'Are we certain this is the right direction? It seems like a very bumpy road'.

How would you respond if you were in the room?

You might have the urge to respond with, 'I think we can handle this, we are well-prepared', maybe accompanied with a slight feeling of annoyance while thinking to yourself, 'bumpiness, what does that even mean?'. The immediate response that signals there is no issue, combined with the skepticism about bumpiness, comes from the left side of your brain. The question could be dismissed instead of leading to a discussion.

But perhaps you would want to dig a little deeper and ask a (right-brain) question such as, 'What kind of bumps are you thinking of?'. Then, the executive who raised the bumpy road has to specify their point. A bumpy road is a metaphoric image for yet-to-be-described difficulties. Specificity or capturing details, can be challenging for the right brain – and the executive's response might well be something quite broad like 'I suspect there will be a lot of resistance among the employees'.

You might then respond with, 'employees are always resistant, it's our job to bring them along, ultimately this is the best for the business'. Or maybe you would follow up with another question to hear more about the employee resistance. In the many business meetings that I have attended, the powerful left brains, including my own, are not patient with anything vague and are all too ready to waltz over the right brain, dismiss its input, and keep going on their own path.

It takes a skilled and experienced listener to notice such moments, and to manage the subsequent discussion to allow the right brain some time to fully crystallize its input so that it can then be integrated into the decision-making process. In the discussion above (derived from a real event) what would have been brought onto the table is that the executive team was about to decide to close a factory and communicate that decision to the employees. The closing of the factory would have taken at least two years and, during that time, they would have had a demotivated, resistant workforce, with a disproportionate amount of sick leave, ultimately becoming a drain on management time and destroying a lot of value. Acknowledging that bumpy road by giving the right brain time to express itself, would have been a wise move allowing issues to be circumvented.

How do we begin to invite the right brain into the conversation? So far, we have learned that we have to communicate via images and we have to manage our left brain's tendency to dismiss right-brain input, inserting some patience into our conversations to allow the right-brain input to be adequately put into words. In Chapter Two we will explore several different techniques to stimulate right-brain participation in our day-to-day discussions and thinking processes.

The unique strengths of the right brain

For the right brain, the present moment is huge, timeless, connected to everything and everybody. Jill Bolte-Taylor, a neuroanatomist who suffered a stroke in her left brain, experienced, at the time, a pure right-brain sensation of the world. She describes it in her TED talk[6] as an energy collage and she writes in her book 'My Stroke of Insight':

> 'Borders between specific entities are softened and complex mental collages can be recalled in their entirety as combinations of images, kinesthetic and physiology'.[7]

Not only does the right brain see a picture, it sees the whole picture.

The ability to see the whole is often referred to as holistic or 'Gestalt' perception. Gestalt is a German word; the closest translation is 'shape' or 'form'. Gestalt perception means the perception of a pattern or structure as a whole, not only individual components, with the inference that the whole is more than the sum of its parts. In the 1950s, Gestalt therapy was developed by Fritz Perls, and has since become a well-established therapeutic approach.[8] Key to this approach is that the therapist works with a patient in the here and now, in the belief that everything that is needed is in the present moment. This is a fundamentally different method to the more traditional psychodynamic therapeutic approaches where looking into past experiences is seen as key to processing and dealing with difficult psychological feelings or reactions. From our current understanding of the brain, we can deduce that Gestalt therapy's philosophy and techniques are focused on working with the right side of the brain. Consequently, in working with the right side of the brain, we can learn from the techniques used in Gestalt therapy. For example, when engaging the right brain it is important to stay in the present moment and to hold off from immediate analyzing or finding connections to past events.

In my coaching sessions, I have found that by engaging the right brain it is possible to capture a complex situation in a single representation, regardless of its long history of details, number of parties involved, conflicting interests, etc. The right brain can indeed see and express a complex whole all at once. The example from the introduction of the vertical rock is an illustration of this. The image captured the essence of what the executive was experiencing in a way that all the verbal information about the situation had not been able to do, exactly like a Gestalt perception where the whole is more than the sum of the parts.

While the right brain is experiencing the entirety of the present moment, the left brain is focused on capturing the moment by reducing its complexity. It puts together details in a linear and methodological way and manifests the concept of time by dividing moments into past, present and future. By defining, structuring and eliminating parts that don't seem relevant, the left brain makes the world tangible, easier to predict and control. One could say the left brain creates a model of reality, which enables us to operate efficiently within that reality. Using the left-brain model of reality has allowed us to build organizations, industries, financial systems and governments.

Each reality, left and right, comes with its strengths and weaknesses. We have already seen that a challenge for the right brain is to participate quickly in discussions. One of the important challenges for the left brain is that it can get stuck in the simplified model of reality that it has created. Information that does not align with its model of reality gets ignored or dismissed. The left brain pays attention to what it already knows. As a result, in most cases, what is new is first experienced in the right brain.[9] This is what makes the right brain so essential when we are stuck in our thinking.

You may remember a time where you couldn't figure out how to get something done. Then while you are doing something entirely different, such as reading the newspaper or glancing at some advertisement, all of a sudden, there is a glimmer of an idea. Or a colleague makes an off-hand comment and you can sense something shifting. It can literally seem like the idea is at the edge of your awareness, and you have to pause to see it and hold on to it, to 'grab' it.

I remember a time when our daughters were very young and we had a beautiful open staircase which was completely unsafe for kids, they could have easily fallen through the bars. I couldn't figure out how to create something safe while preserving the atmosphere of an open space. For hours, I unsuccessfully hunted the internet for an answer. A few days later, while watching a sailing race, I suddenly saw my stairs were a bit like the railing of a sailing yacht. Shortly after, with a bit more internet searching, options for child-safe yacht railings provided an excellent solution for our stairs while preserving the lovely feeling of the open space.

The right brain's capacity to see the new is especially invaluable when dealing with the kind of problems where it feels like you are going in circles. In conversations, I have often been astonished by the right-brain ability to express the whole, see a glimpse of something new and support someone to find a way forward in highly complex situations. It feels a bit like magic. Chapter Three discusses several practical ways of accessing these unique strengths of the right brain.

The right brain is also highly relevant for our personal and professional development, and consequently to coaching. For those of you who are less familiar with the field of coaching - a good definition of coaching is, 'The art of facilitating the development, learning and performance of another'.[10] Without exception coaching conversations are about exploring the new, including new ways of leading, new perspectives, and new behaviors which makes involving the right side of the brain essential.

communicates in words

like a serial processor; methodical, linear, and logical

sees the parts it recognizes as 'relevant'

captures, details, and labels the world in a model

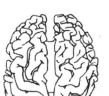

communicates in images

like a parallel processor; holistic and simultaneous

sees the whole

experiences everything, including what is new

Both left- and right-brain realities are essential to us and it would clearly be to our benefit for both sides to collaborate. Imagine an iterative process where we start with the right-brain holistic perception of a situation, and then allow the left brain to utilize and shape it, to fill in the details and identify what actions to take. Then we bring in the right brain again to sense check. But here is the catch. The right side of the brain collaborates easily and naturally with the left, but not vice versa. Recalling the earlier discussion on how the left brain can dismiss the right brain's input, this is perhaps not so surprising. Once the left brain gets the ball, it keeps it to itself and an increasingly left-brain world becomes a self-reinforcing reality.

Thankfully, the right hemisphere has a proverbial ace up its sleeve.

The right brain as a source of wisdom about ourselves and others

The right side of our brain is considered vital for emotional recognition and emotional expression. It is seen as the center of our capacity for empathy, the ability to share and understand the emotions of others, and is therefore essential to our social lives. While there is traction for the view that we are living in an increasingly left-brain world, it seems to me that humanity is not giving up its emotional and social life anytime soon. Experiencing the unbridled happiness of people getting together after the pandemic lockdowns – teenagers, young adults, executives and senior folks alike – is a case in point.

How is the right brain connected to our emotional experiences and social lives? Interestingly, the connection comes through the body. You may know that the motor neurons of the left brain direct the right side of the body, and vice versa. Moving your right arm is done by the left side of your brain. However, the information from the whole of your body flows via the brainstem into the right side of your brain.[11] This means that an image of the whole body is mapped only in the right side of the brain, including any awareness of our internal bodily state through organs like the heart, the lungs and the gut.

This kind of information from the body is the physical representation, or embodiment, of our emotions. Emotions we feel are how the brain interprets physical signals from the body. For example, when our hearts start to race, our muscles contract and our mouth runs dry, we usually interpret that as fear. Context and surroundings matters to how the brain interprets information from the body. In a telling experiment, a group of men was invited to walk over a wobbly rope bridge while another group walked over a solid bridge. Both groups were met by an attractive interviewer at the end of the bridge who asked a series of questions. Though the interviewer behaved in a similar manner towards both groups, many more members of the first group attempted post-experimental contact with the interviewer. They interpreted part of their increased heartrate and sweaty palms as attraction, instead of merely fear from crossing the rope bridge.[12]

People are very different in how they experience emotions. Some have a rich, at times even overwhelming, presence of emotions in their life whereas others are less in touch with their emotional experience. Think about the connection between the right brain and the body as a door that can be fully open, fully closed or anything in between. For those that experience emotions fully, the door is very open. For those that find it hard to answer a question like 'how do you feel', the door is less open. Our history, upbringing and personal experience play a big part in how open this particular door is.

Just over twenty years ago, Dr. Giacomo Rizzolatti discovered the existence of mirror neurons.[13] These neurons are activated when observing an action by someone else. When one person at a table takes a glass of water, many others experience a dry throat and then reach for the water themselves. When you approach a group of laughing people, the corners of your mouth will turn up and your eyes will crinkle. When I watch speed skating on television, a favorite in my home country The Netherlands, my body starts swaying from left to right. When we see a loved one suffering, our own eyes fill with tears, sometimes even before we know what is going on. Scientists wondered for many years why we respond to each other so vividly. Mirror neurons finally provided an explanation. Through these neurons we have a physical experience that mirrors what the other person is experiencing and, as described above, we attach an emotion to those physical sensations.

In other words, the experience of our own emotions as well as the emotions of others, the basis of empathy, is directly related to the connection between the whole body and the right side of the brain. This is the essence of the importance of our right brain for our emotional and social lives. Note that the experience of emotions is subjective, our interpretation of body information is dependent on factors such as context, personal history and surroundings. In the left brain's model of reality, emotions have little place (remember the left brain tends to dismiss right-brain input) which makes the left-brain experience of the world more objective and rational.

This all means that the right brain, through the body, often has a knowledge and wisdom about our emotional and social lives that our left brain does not yet have. And it is possible for us to tap into this wisdom. For example, there are many instances in language that connect our bodies with our emotional life to convey information, such as, 'I am sitting on the fence', or, 'my head is in the clouds', or to ask for information, 'where do you stand on this matter?'. In a discussion, we might say, 'can you step into my shoes for a moment and look at it from my perspective?'. This sentence can shift an entire conversation in an instance (though no-one is exchanging footwear).

It becomes even more intriguing when we can uncover new information by actively involving our bodies. In one of our leadership workshops we do an exercise called perceptual positions. Participants are asked to consider a working relationship where they see room for improvement. We take three pieces of paper, label them 1, 2 and 3, and put them on the floor. Paper 1 represents the participant, Paper 2 represents the other party involved and Paper 3 represents a fly on the wall. Stepping on the different pieces of paper generates surprising insights into improving the working relationship.

There is a wealth of body information at any given moment, yet we are not very good at tuning in to this type of information nor very proficient in understanding it. In Chapter Four we look at several pragmatic ways to get started with tapping into this wisdom of the right brain.

communicates in words

communicates in images

like a serial processor; methodical, linear, and logical

like a parallel processor; holistic and simultaneous

sees the parts it recognises as 'relevant'

sees the whole

captures, details, and labels the world in a model

experiences everything, including what is new

sense of time

sense of the whole body

deeper connection to the objective and rational

deeper connection to the emotional and social

While the right brain experiences a connection with others through the body, it also strongly experiences disconnection. As mentioned in the introduction, it may have happened to you that you were listening to someone and, although what they said sounded logical, you just did not believe them. In case of doubt, the emotions generated by the receipt of body information through the right brain always have the higher priority in our internal evaluation[14]. In addition, what is important to know is that the body always responds the fastest[15]. In a negotiation, if your thinking is leading you to say yes, your body, which includes your face, is probably already showing it and vice versa. It takes a lot of practice to have what we call a 'poker face' where your true feelings don't show on your face. Furthermore, no information is a negative for your brain so unless there is a good explanation for a lack of expression, such as playing an actual poker game, we tend not to trust people who lack facial expression.

Earlier, we saw that the right brain needs imagery to communicate, some patience to translate its insights into words, and staying in the present moment. In addition, to be comfortably present in a conversation, the right brain also needs to experience 'we'. To give a simple illustration; a conversation sitting opposite someone at a conference table is a very different encounter from having the same conversation while taking a walk together. You will most likely have come across this many times yourself. When we walk next to each other, we are moving forward together while our conversation unfolds. If we disagree, we keep walking together, the 'we' experience continues, and we discuss our differences. When sitting in a meeting room opposite one another, we are easily hooked into being adversaries, even on small things, and we can become polarized and stuck in that dynamic.

In business meetings, when a discussion gets challenging, someone might pick up a pen and walk to the flip chart to draw or write something to illustrate what they mean. Everyone is then looking together at the piece of paper and that immediately impacts the atmosphere, which often becomes more collaborative as a result. In coaching sessions, the coach needs to facilitate right-brain participation and then create a place, a playing field, for collaboration between the left and the right side of the brain of their coachees. This can only happen in the presence of this 'we' experience.

When I first wrote this part of the book, it suddenly occurred to me that everything I have read, learned and experienced illustrates the deep competence of the left brain and the infinite wisdom of the right brain. Unexpectedly, I was feeling tearful as I wrote this sentence, filled with a mix of wonder and sadness at the same time.

It also felt immediately rather silly and irrelevant to write this down. I hesitated. The left brain can quickly come across as judging and belittling even though I am not sure whether that is its intent. It might be frustration from not understanding something in the way the right brain does and therefore ridicule is its defense. Isn't that what we often do in our interactions with others when we don't understand something? Though the widely held view that we live in an increasingly left-brain world is convincing and suggests that the left brain is on the winning side of the hemispheric power struggle, I maintain a sense of optimism about the strength, wisdom and power of the right side of our brains.

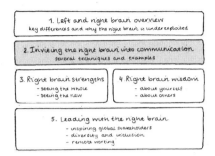

1. Left and right brain overview
key differences and why the right brain is under exploited

2. Inviting the right brain into communication
several techniques and examples

3. Right brain strengths
- seeing the whole
- seeing the new

4. Right brain wisdom
- about yourself
- about others

5. Leading with the right brain
- inspiring global stakeholders
- diversity and inclusion
- remote working

Inviting the right brain into our communication

'What is most on my mind is how to set up things well for this new project'. Karen is a partner in a management consulting firm and has just brought in a six-week project with a large new client. It's 2020 and lockdowns abound. With many team members struggling remotely, Karen finds it challenging to manage them as well as her own working hours. With the additional complication of having young children at home, she is feeling the strain on her well-being.

We start by discussing what would tell her that things are working well for the new project. Karen mentions a couple of pointers such as energized, engaged team members and clients, collaborative team discussions and good individual learning.

'Can you find a picture that would illustrate this successful state?', I ask, showing her a collection of pictures (more on this later). Karen selects the following image:[16]

She explains that, while there is a lot going on in the picture, the combination of colors, structure, and the general sense of lightness in the illustration all represent to her a successful project.

Furthermore, the different patterns on each side of the rainbow are especially relevant in that the project is like a new world for her team to operate in, where they need to change their ways of working.

'So, where are you in this image?', I ask next.

Karen reflects that she could quite naturally be the person crawling through the rainbow, connecting the different worlds, but also that this is perhaps not what she should be doing. It is a familiar role, one where she would be actively involved in the work, and she knows she is up to this. Still, she is wondering if this is the right choice for her. We explore together what else could represent her role. She lights up when contemplating the idea that she could be the sun. After all what makes the picture work for her is its lightness and color. Karen considers that the sun representing her in this context would mean bringing the team vision, positivity, hope and warmth – powerful yet with a bit more distance – elements she is keen to embrace.

As the coaching session progresses, the image also helps her to visualize the roles and responsibilities of other team members, and her own responsibility in supporting them. In our subsequent conversations, we keep referring to the image and how she is fulfilling her role. Karen mentions how, for example, she is asking more open questions, suggesting areas to explore instead of sharing strong hypotheses, giving the team confidence by celebrating successes and making sure there is enough fun in the meetings. Karen also tells me she has printed the picture and stuck it on her desk as a daily reminder of what she wants her role to be when interacting with the team.

As in the example above, this chapter will demonstrate a number of visual techniques to evoke images and thereby invite the right side of the brain into a conversation. It is helpful to have multiple tools at your disposal to do so – they keep the discourse fresh and interesting. These techniques can be used in all kinds of conversations, from a portfolio discussion between executives to a chat with a friend, as well as a development meeting at work or even a formal coaching session. We will explore the following visual techniques and review the general principles of how to apply each in a conversation:

- Pictures
- Metaphors (free)
- Metaphors (guided)
- Objects
- Drawing

For executive coaches, this chapter and the following ones contain grey boxes with more detail on how to use a specific tool or approach in a coaching session.

The question I am often asked is 'Isn't this all a bit too playful... does a senior executive really take you seriously if you bring out a stack of pictures or a box full of objects to illustrate a situation'. I can confidently say, after fifteen years of doing this, that it is the most senior clients who are often the most intrigued to be given a different way to explore an issue. They have typically already thought and reflected on so many aspects of their situation that asking questions does not surface much new information for them. When opening my box of objects, they are interested, curious and immediately have a smile on their face. Some might say, 'But I am really not good at drawing', when asked to put pen to paper. A simple assurance that anything on the paper will be fine, including circles and stick figures, usually takes care of any such resistance.

What is perhaps good to note is that, in a discussion or a coaching session, I don't give my client the choice of which visual tool to use; they wouldn't know how to choose. This is my responsibility as I am facilitating the process of our discussion. Outside a formal coaching session, especially if you are working with someone who is familiar with right-brain tools – you can discuss together what tool to use or you can also simply introduce something. It is more relevant to do something that ignites the right brain, rather than try to find the best option.

Pictures

Pictures are one of the most versatile visual tools to stimulate the right brain. They can be used for many different purposes such as describing a situation, a person, a feeling, a relationship, a vision, etc. Some people are naturally visual in their use of language and easily talk in images, often referred to as metaphors (i.e. 'it's a whirlwind around here' or 'I am dragging my feet'). Working with metaphors is also a very useful way of accessing the right brain and will be covered in the next part of the chapter. However, if your client or colleague never uses metaphor in their speech, chances are they will struggle when you suddenly ask them for one. In that case, a set of suitable images are a very useful tool. I have not met a coachee yet who could not find an image to illustrate their situation from a set of pictures.

In certain business areas it is already an established technique to use pictures. Marketing teams may ask focus groups to select pictures they associate with corporate brands, or to make a brand collage from magazines. Formal business presentations have increasingly more visuals. In my own earlier work as a strategy consultant at The Boston Consulting Group, we were trained in the art of making a powerful slide. The slides most remembered by clients were never the ones with many words but rather the ones with strong images, in the form of graphs or other visuals. Today, when I bring out a set of pictures, more often than not the client will say, 'we use these too in product design, marketing, training, etc.'. Typically, though, organizations use pictures only for specific purposes, like focus groups. The step we are taking now is bringing pictures deliberately into one-to-one and team conversations.

Next time you meet a new team member, ask them to find a picture to illustrate their leadership style or their way of working to you. Or maybe ask a colleague in the middle of a tricky situation to select a picture that represents the challenge. See how much more you understand the situation through their eyes when you look at their chosen pictures.

In team discussions, pictures can fast-track building connections, create good energy or resolve differences. For example, by asking team members to find a picture...

...describing what energizes them.

...describing when the team works well together and/or when it doesn't.

...illustrating what brings them to work every day; why they do what they do.

...describing the level of pressure they are experiencing at the moment.

The resulting conversations are not typically any longer than those without pictures, but they have a different quality. Attentive listening and curious questions come more naturally, generating relevant insight and collaboration. People seem to navigate more easily to common ground when looking at each other's pictures, which I see as a consequence of the 'we' experience that the right brain evokes.

To use pictures regularly, having a set at hand is a necessity. As a starting facilitator and coach, I invested in a set of images called *The Visual Explorer*.[17] The size of a pack of playing cards, they have travelled with me across the world and been part of countless conversations with individuals and teams. In the appendix is an overview of different pictures sets and where to find them.

The reflections or emotions these images evoke do not need to be comfortable and positive. On the contrary, it is often easier for someone to express a difficult truth visually than in words.

I recall a conversation where a new client, let's call him Paul, begins with, 'I am not enjoying work very much at the moment'.

How does one interpret that statement? Is it a bit too busy at work or something more serious? We can ask a few more questions such as 'what do you mean, can you tell me more?' but it still might be difficult to calibrate the situation, especially if you don't know the person that well. In this case, I ask Paul to find a picture to illustrate how he experiences work and he picks this one:[18]

What happens to you when you look at this image? Personally, I immediately feel something visceral in my chest and throat, accompanied by a strong feeling of dread.

Knowing about the connection between the right brain and the body, this strong physical reaction is not unexpected even if it does pack an uncomfortable punch. And, while my brain quickly interprets these strong sensations as a feeling of dread, I am not sure at this point if Paul's physical sensations are the same as mine or, even if they are, whether he attaches a similar feeling to those sensations. Yet what we do have is this richness of information, stimulated by the picture, that we can talk about.

'That is a strong image,' I say, putting my hand on my chest, 'I feel it immediately here, in my chest, when I look at that'. 'What is your reaction?'

Paul responds that he mostly feels a sensation in his gut, a churning that is constantly there at work. We talk about the emotions involved and Paul says he is experiencing everything at work in a negative way. 'Sometimes', he shares, 'I know a discussion is rationally fine or a comment is meant constructively, but for me it is all annoying and I keep thinking about just quitting. But I also know this is not a smart move as I don't know what else I want to do.'

I ask Paul whether he is able to afford, financially, to leave his role without anything else lined up.

'Not really', Paul replies, 'and the thought of doing that makes me feel very stressed.'

At this point, I share my feeling of dread, and my concern for his well-being. He smiles and says he is quite fine because at home he is feeling very different. Though the work situation is unpleasant, it is not defining his overall well-being. I notice I am still feeling skeptical and ask Paul to choose a picture to illustrate how he feels at home: [19]

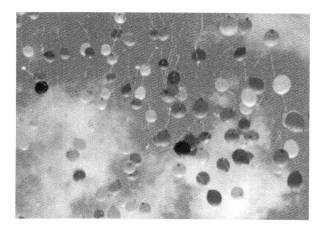

Naturally this picture evokes a very different reaction in me, as presumably it does for you, too. I feel myself relaxing, instinctively understanding the big difference he referred to earlier, and trusting that, at least for now, he is managing.

Our conversation starts to focus on the differences between work and home. Paul knows that making a big decision, such as leaving his job, whilst being in a very negative place is risky. The brain picks up the signals from our environment that confirm our negative bias and we get stuck in the 'glass half empty' way of looking at the world. Paul is willing to do a short experiment to influence his perspective and get to more neutral place.

Repeated experiments have shown that we can help bring ourselves to a more balanced viewpoint by committing to writing down at the end of the day three good things about that day.[20] The aim is not to look at the world through rose-colored glasses but to avoid being trapped in a perpetual negative state of mind. Those who do this exercise report a change in their experience of reality within a three-week period. It's a powerful mechanism and it works very well for Paul – at our next coaching session four weeks later he walks in with a more balanced and realistic view on his workplace, which then allows us to start a constructive discussion on how he wants to shape his career.

Through pictures, our right brain, our bodies and our feelings become part of the fabric of the conversation. It doesn't matter that in that first meeting with Paul, my responses are in my chest and not in my gut as Paul's are. The important thing is that I am responding, both physically and emotionally, to what he is communicating to me through the picture. This resonance builds trust and connection fast. Furthermore, by allowing the picture to represent how hard work was, Paul could talk about these difficulties with a bit of distance. Often, the fear of being overwhelmed by our emotions holds us back from being accurate about them. A picture can bring the severity of the situation across without that overwhelm. This small bit of distance – of perspective – between ourselves and our emotions can be the first step towards change.

As a leader, when one of your team members is in such a negative state of mind, it is essential to realize that they are completely stuck. Any suggestions or solutions you offer them will, at best, simply bounce off them and, at worst, widen the gap between you and even reinforce that they are not well-suited for the job. By bringing your right brain into the interaction, strengthening trust and giving them the tools to move away from the negative mindset, you create the opportunity for a different outcome. You enable a team member to be at their best.

A few key pointers for bringing pictures into conversations:

- Formulate a very simple question for selecting a picture. It doesn't matter if the question is not perfect – the right brain knows what's relevant and it will select a relevant image. Trust the process.
- Get someone talking about their picture – what do they see when they look at it, what does it illustrate? Turn on your curiosity, that is all you need. There is no right or wrong answer or reflection on this input. As an aside - please don't ask 'why did you pick this one' – the word 'why' makes all of us defensive which is not a good starting point.
- Offer your own reactions and ideas in an open way. Don't shy away from offering your responses but don't lead with them. Treat your responses as data or input, not as conclusions.
- Have a laugh together.

Metaphors - free

Let's look next at invoking images and inviting the right brain through the use of metaphors, within the spoken word rather than through pictures.

One of the founders of a tech company, Sarah, a year into the pandemic, had saved the company by taking it over from her partners and keeping it afloat herself.

'You know', she says, 'we ended the year in the black and I was really proud of that. I had also made some steps in finding a new partner, John, and making him an offer to join the company. Then, everything went haywire.' She proceeds to explain that John needed surgery and had by now been bedridden for a while. 'It is an awful situation for John. I fully understand he is not in a position to make substantial professional decisions and I want to support him. At the same time, and I feel a bit selfish saying this, I have noticed I am feeling increasingly uncomfortable myself. We have not yet even discussed the offer, even though it is now over two months since I made it. It is a bit like I took off my clothes when I made that offer, opened up my books, and didn't get a response'.

'Right,' I say, 'so you have been standing there without any clothes on for two months…'

'Exactly', she continues, 'and I am beginning to feel a little chilly. Actually, extremely chilly.'

I shake my shoulders, 'I am feeling the chill', I say, 'What else is happening, are you standing there by yourself?'

'Yes', Sarah confirms, 'the room is empty and I am just waiting, and getting colder and colder'

Many of you, leaders and coaches alike, will be familiar with the power of a good metaphor. Whether going after some low-hanging fruit, riding out the financial storm, boiling the ocean or winning the battle – metaphors are often used in business conversations.

Metaphors access the right brain in the same way that pictures do. And, very practically, it does not require anything special like a picture set. In a coaching session, when someone talks easily in metaphors, like Sarah, the coach can simply expand what is being offered. I refer to this as the 'free' metaphor. The role of the coach is to capture the image and make it more visible. Once visible, the image can be part of the coaching session in exactly the same way as a picture. This is equally true for any other conversation, at work or beyond. Someone might naturally say, 'this just feels heavy' when referring to a piece of work. A little prompt like, 'heavy, tell me more, what kind of heavy…?', can already invite the right brain to elaborate.

With Sarah, the next part of our coaching session centered on how to be less cold, for example by grabbing a towel or putting on a bathrobe. She said she really wanted a bathrobe, something warm and more permanent. She didn't need to get dressed properly but a towel was insufficient. We then explored what a bathrobe would represent in the actual situation. She decided to ask John if he could engage with the offer now or else she would table it for six months. Then, she would revisit and make a new offer if appropriate. This practical approach gave her back a feeling of control, she proceeded to speak with John and consequently tabled the offer for six months.

In one of our subsequent conversations, I inquire, 'what's the situation with John, are you still chilly?'

'Not at all', Sarah replies, 'I am now fully dressed, nice and warm, it's good.'

In a conversation, once the metaphor is established, both parties can freely contribute to shaping it. Last week, one of my coachees, reflecting on his leadership skills, said that he was a good captain and was skilled in recruiting people to join his crew. Yet in his recent role, he had to influence many senior people who didn't want to serve on his ship. He was finding that some of his 'crew recruiting skills' were not helpful for influencing these senior stakeholders. I offered him the image of a fleet and suggested influencing senior stakeholders may be more like convincing other captains to join the fleet with their own ships rather than subjecting to his command on his ship. This resonated and we continued to explore why other captains would join a fleet and how to convince them.

In conversations with metaphors, the approach is simple: give the person who offers the metaphor some time to expand on it. Then, feel free to contribute your own ideas. Often the easiest first step is to play back the metaphor. As with Sarah, 'so you have been standing there without clothes for two months...'. By playing back the words, the other person will continue their train of thought and you avoid influencing the image too early, just as Sarah continued her train of thought by saying, 'I am feeling chilly'.

Then, you can get into the metaphor with them which empathizes the 'we' experience and further strengthens the right brain presence, like my words, 'I am feeling the chill' and shaking my shoulders. By the way, faking your response immediately destroys the connection. In the same way that deliberately mirroring body language when listening to someone can come across as disingenuous – so can faking the metaphor experience feel false. You have to truly see the metaphor in your own mind's eye and experience it physically. This is a good example of leading with your right brain; stepping into someone else's world and living that moment with them.

Once the image is clear, it is a good idea to explore within the metaphor what to do next - such as putting on the bathrobe in Sarah's example or exploring how other captains would join the fleet. When the next step in the metaphor is clear, then link back to the actual situation and explore together what that step in the metaphoric world represents in the real world. For Sarah, this meant asking John whether he could engage with her offer now, or she would table it for six months.

In another conversation someone compared their situation to being in the eye of the storm. In that case, the next step would be to explore what we can do when we are in the eye of the storm (take shelter, get out of there, etc.) – the right brain has remarkable intuition about what to do within the image. This is quick and fun to explore, and then gives actionable steps in the real world.

Metaphors - guided

Even though the power of image resides in all of us - we all have a right side of our brain - not everyone easily thinks and talks in metaphors. So this is where we can help to guide someone into a particular type of metaphor. Earlier, we explored the metaphor of a landscape, the vertical cliff face that Marc felt he was scaling. Other useful guided metaphors include asking what color, music, sports, city, drink, or animal comes to mind when thinking about a person or situation.

The story, below, is taken from a conversation where we used color to guide the metaphor:

Liza, about to take on a new role, acknowledges that her main challenge is to shift part of her focus from running projects towards business development. This realization is not new to her, yet she is finding it hard to make this shift and has been thinking about it for a while. I ask her what color she associates with her current role.

'Purple', she replies, 'I love purple and all of its different shades'.

'And what color is the new role to you'

'Orange', is her immediate reply.

This is an interesting moment in the conversation for me. Being Dutch, orange has a specific meaning as anyone who has seen Dutch supporters at a sport event, or pictures of King's day in The Netherlands, will understand. I am immediately flooded with the big Dutch orange feeling, a very positive one. However, I need to understand Liza's. 'So, what is your view on orange?', I ask her.

'It's an aggressive color, not one of my favorites', she says while making a face that illustrates the dislike. 'Ok', I mumble while nodding, inviting her to speak more while I let go of my instant desire to argue about the beauty of orange. 'I never wear anything orange, don't have it in my house, just don't like it', Liza continues.

Truth be told, I can't resist a tiny push back on this orange assault. 'What strikes me about orange is that it is a mix of yellow and red', I offer.

'Ah', she says, 'that is interesting, I actually really like yellow, it's bright, light, very motivating and energizing. The yellow speaks to me a lot. It's the red that represents stress and pressure.'

My thoughts go back to purple, and how purple is a mix of blue and red. I ask, 'Is that the same red?'.

'Yes', she says and adds on reflection, 'and the blue represents my calm. After running projects for many years, I bring a lot of calm and experience. I know I am good at this. Team members and clients have commented on my ability to stay calm in difficult moments and manage the situation.' We reflect together that this perhaps suggests that the yellow needs to become stronger to balance the red, in the same way that the blue balances the red.

At this point, our time is almost done, and I know Liza has a hard stop for our conversation. I ask her what has resonated most about the color exploration.

'Discovering the yellow in business development', she replies. As we have to finish, we agree she will reflect what yellow represents in the context of business development and will try to approach upcoming client development meetings from the yellow angle.

This sounds rather vague as a next step but the right brain doesn't need a very specific instruction to keep processing. As mentioned in the introduction, once such a new right brain perspective has been captured, we cannot un-know it and it can be that the previously identified issue simply evaporates. In Liza's case, she continued working on additional skills for business development, which was a normal learning process in her new role.

The principles and pointers for using guided metaphors are the same as for free metaphors – we give the metaphor some attention so it becomes clearly visible in both our minds, then investigate what is happening in the metaphor before translating back to the situation at hand.

The guided metaphor is most powerful when specifically connected to the coachee's life. For example, by linking into a hobby or interest. A coachee many years ago was a passionate motorcyclist and during one of our sessions, we discussed what kind of road he was biking along and which skills he needed to maximize his enjoyment of the drive.

Recently, in conversation with another client, James, we explored how he could use metaphors in his context as a leader. James had joined a new organization in the middle of the pandemic and so far had only worked with colleagues and clients via Zoom. He knew he had established his credibility based on his knowledge and experience, yet he felt restricted in expanding those connections, especially during virtual meetings with people who had previously met each other in person. We discussed the concept of connecting via the right brain and he wanted to experiment. A few weeks later he reported that communicating through metaphors worked well for him. He had noticed that, with a few exceptions, many people easily engaged with the metaphor and others started bringing their own metaphors into the conversation. He also observed that metaphors can come back in subsequent meetings, they tend to hang around in people's memories. When a metaphor is revisited, it can create a really positive feeling of connection and relationship.

Objects

Before reading on, take a moment to look around you and locate an object in your surroundings that symbolizes something about you. Follow your instinct and focus on the first object that speaks to you.

Close your eyes for a moment and imagine sharing the story of what this object says about you with a colleague or friend. What quality of yours does this object illustrate? Now consider how this quality is present in your leadership style?

This small exercise resembles what I often do during a workshop or meeting to allow people to quickly connect with each other in a rich way.

Let's see how objects can work in an in-person conversation.

Philippe is responsible for operations in a fast-growing company. He has recently stepped into the role and become part of the management team. While he enjoys the new responsibility, he finds it hard to contribute to the Management Team (MT) discussions and he wants to use our coaching session to work on strengthening his presence and impact in the MT. He mentions immediately that he is not very good at engaging others. 'Usually I am quite flat,' he says.

'So,' I reply, 'what do you have that you can build on i.e. parts of your personality, like strengths or qualities, that are a foundation of who you are? Take a moment to reflect while I get something from my bag.' With these words I put a small box of objects on the table, roughly spreading them out.

Phillipe laughs and asks what they are. I reply that they can be helpful to illustrate qualities, 'and it's fun to work with them. Are you ok to try that?' Philippe nods. 'Great, so please find some objects, just two or three, that illustrate your qualities or strengths that you can build on.'

He selects a stone, a dice and a conker. As a first step, we discuss each object, the quality it represents and explore together how he could use that quality to engage others in the MT meetings.

Most surprising is how he sees himself in relation to the dice, 'I know I can take calculated gambles,' he says, 'it is a part of my personality that not many people see'.

'Calculated gambles in what way?' I ask, 'Can you give me an example?'.

'Mm,' he says, ' I can't think of anything right now'

'Ok, maybe can you think of someone who is like that too?'

Philippe smiles and says, 'Well, it's like that Jordan character in *'The Wolf of Wall Street'*,[21] playing poker and such. Although, of course, I would do nothing illegal'. We both laugh, Jordan's character is such a contrast to Phillipe's modest, calm appearance.

'So what would Jordan do in your MT meetings,' I ask.

Philippe thinks about that for a moment and replies, 'He would not stay in his comfort zone, he would put topics on the table and ask questions.'.

Following his flow, I continue, 'So in your last MT, what topics or questions might Jordan have put on the table?'

Now Phillipe identifies a few specific things and then we discuss what will be on the agenda for the next MT meetings and what he might like to bring up. We identify concrete actions including relevant examples to introduce, pertinent questions to ask, and colleagues to connect with beforehand to understand their views.

As we talk about how to release his inner Jordan to increase his presence in the MT meetings, our discussion is animated and full of energy, and leads to key practical next steps. This conversation, I point out to him, feels like a good illustration of the energy he can bring into the MT meetings. We take some time to capture this sensation of energy – physically, mentally and emotionally. This opens a broader topic for us to explore about how this energy is part of his life, where he can access it most easily and what else he would like to do with this energy.

Objects are particularly useful to represent people or different parts of a person. For example, an object to represent your boss and an object to represent you. Or an object for the part of you that likes the new job and the part of you that doesn't like the new job.

When using objects in a conversation, the same pointers apply as mentioned earlier for pictures and metaphors. I would like to emphasize again how important it is to trust the right brain to bring what is relevant. With Philippe, I was deliberately vague with the question: 'Find two or three objects that represent qualities that you can build on'. It would have been easy to say, '...qualities that you can build for your presence in the MT' but I didn't want to be too specific, knowing this would likely activate his strong analytical left brain. He had been clear at the start he would like to work on his presence in the MT so his brain already had this as the context.

When meeting someone in person, I often carry a small box of objects and it has become a particular favorite tool in my coaching sessions as it is such a playful yet impactful way of working. For virtual conversations, I have created a slide depicting different objects, which has been an equally cherished companion.

Even without an object box or an object slide, it is entirely possible to work in this way as there are always useable objects in your surroundings, even in a meeting room.

Before the pandemic, I would have said that objects were quite a specialized tool for in-person conversations but working with objects is actually remarkably suitable for virtual meetings. Sharing objects via the screen can tangibly shift the atmosphere in a virtual discussion.

Recently during a virtual conversation with someone who was sitting outside, we had identified several options as to how he could proceed in a challenging situation. I asked him what he was seeing around him that was somehow connected to each option. He identified a small creek for option 1, a bin for option 2 and a very large tree behind him for option 3. Not surprisingly, he was not keen to do option 2. The large tree represented a forceful approach that he knew was possible yet was not forward-looking. The most appealing was the creek as it highlighted setting something in motion beyond the immediate situation and beyond himself. Noting this desire to set something in motion was a new insight for him.

Flow of a coaching session with images or objects

- Open the discussion by connecting with your coachee and establishing a topic and/or objective for the session. This does not need to be done in great detail yet is it important to set a context for the right brain input.

- To introduce the visual way of working, you can simply ask them, 'Are you up for exploring this topic in a different way?'

- Formulate a very simple question to get started. Trust the right brain to know what is relevant rather than finding the perfect question.

- Sometimes the coachee will say that they don't understand the question. It can certainly happen that your question was too vague, but this is usually their left brain kicking in to distract and redirect their attention. When this happens, I will say something like, 'Yes, my question was a bit vague; please pick a picture/ object that is relevant for our conversation, if it's not completely clear why just pick something that speaks to you'. In most cases, this takes care of the left-brain interference. Yet, sometimes, the left brain is more persistent and insists on more clarification. In that case, you need to lower the barrier even more to allow the right brain in. You can do that, for example, by saying, 'We are looking for an image that describes the situation, so let's have a look through the pictures/objects to see if there is something, otherwise we'll leave it.' In this case, I am making the question as broad as possible and I am speaking in 'we'.

- Ask the coachee to describe what they see and don't hesitate to ask what else comes to mind or probe in a different way. Like Phillipe who didn't have an example of a calculated risk but then came up with the Jordan character. In these second or even third iterations, there is often very valuable information.

- Then, feel free to add your own observations – but offer them purely as suggestions. With Karen, I offered, 'I am wondering if the sun has something to do with your role, the light ….'. She might have found it presumptuous to describe herself as the sun. If the coachee says they don't think your observation is relevant - drop it. Even if you are absolutely convinced your idea is important, they are indicating they are not ready to pick it up. If it is, indeed, important, it will pop up again later – their right brain might have noticed it anyway even if they don't yet acknowledge it.

- Follow the natural flow of the conversation and keep using the visuals. When an idea arrives, explore how it would show up in the image or impact the objects.

- Use the last ten minutes to deliberately invite the left brain into the conversation, to connect the discussion to the objectives from the coaching session. What does this exploration suggest or imply about the coaching objective? What are appropriate next steps? Is there anything else the coachee would like to capture?

We have now seen several examples of the right brain capability to express what is important, leading to new perspectives and insights. The final technique that invites the right side of the brain to participate is drawing, and we will look at a conversation with Michael.

Drawing

'It is crazy busy,' Michael starts our first conversation after the summer holidays, 'and about to get busier. This is a good thing, the period before the summer was a bit slow and the next few months will drive our revenues for the year. It is all work for our main customers and work we need to be doing, but it is several key projects at the same time. I am concerned about being too fragmented, lots of travel, overseeing all the workstreams, continuing to develop the leadership team.' He takes a deep breath.

'Ok', I say, 'so is that what we are focusing on today?'. Michael replies with a heartfelt yes and elaborates that he wants to establish priorities and a sense of control over what is descending over him.

'Tell me more about these different projects, and while you do so, let's open the Zoom Whiteboard so you can also put the pieces on there.'

'How do you mean?' Michael asks.

'See, on the Zoom Whiteboard, you can draw like this', I show him how to annotate. 'Can you draw the projects like squares, or blocks, and size them to show how big they are?'.

A big advantage of drawing is that you can find a pen and a piece of paper just about anywhere. Meeting rooms have flip charts or white boards. I also often carry a small set of felt tips around and some A4 white paper. Bringing out the felt tips puts a smile on people's face – it gives off a 'let's play' vibe. Zoom and other video conferencing platforms have whiteboards too, though they are less playful. When using those, make sure to keep it simple.

Michael draws his projects in the following way. 'Mm,' he says, 'this is clearly not going to add up. What I know for sure is that project B will be 2–2.5 days a week for the foreseeable future, project D will have to be smaller'. After looking at the boxes a moment longer he adds, 'This is making me see that my role has to be different for each of the projects and I have to be very clear on that to the project teams'.

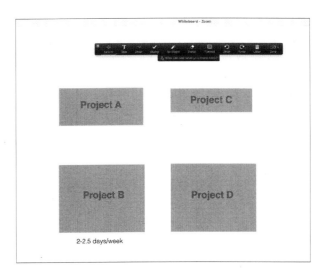

We proceed to discuss his role on each project as well as high-level time allocation for the rest of the year. Michael sees that project A will take 50% of his time for a two-week period and he will only be able to manage that if he preloads work for project D. Project C turns out to be an interesting piece of the puzzle and could either be painful or the cherry on the cake. It has the potential to be an energizing and fun piece of work if Michael carves out a supervising role for himself and delegates the execution. He identifies whom to align with and what to agree on responsibilities to create the right set up from the get go. After another twenty minutes of conversation, the Zoom Whiteboard looks quite different and Michael is smiling, 'I know this will be really busy but it is also exciting'.

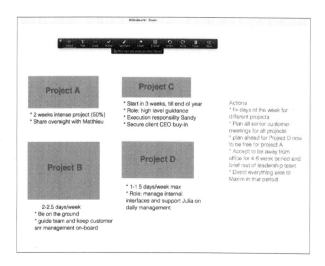

Drawing works particularly well to illustrate a complicated situation with a lot of history and facts, where the essence can be difficult to summarize in a few words. It can naturally focus the mind and conversation, possibly because it is impossible to illustrate all the details in the same way that we can with words.

Inviting the right brain into the conversation – the key concepts

Why might we want to bring visual techniques into a regular conversation? In short, visuals stimulate right-brain activity and participation. The left brain is a powerful problem-solving machine but it can get stuck in its own thinking. Anything new is first experienced in the right brain so bringing the right brain into the conversation can generate new input and fresh perspectives.

We can invite the right brain to participate with pictures, metaphors, objects or drawings. By making something visible, we can look at the image together, stimulating the 'we' experience and further strengthening the right brain input. The flow of such a conversation is roughly the same, regardless of what kind of visual technique you use:

- Identify the issue you are talking about
- Suggest looking at it from a different angle and bring in a visual technique
- Flesh out the visual, take some time to really see and experience the image
- Look for a good next step in the visual
  (such as putting on a bathrobe in an earlier example)
- Translate this next step to real world, to address the issue

One of the key challenges for new leaders and new coaches alike is finding an appropriate balance between using their own thoughts, ideas and experiences and those of the team member/coachee in the discussion (the one with the issue). Often this is referred to as the balance between push and pull or directive and indirective. New leaders and coaches can be pushy with their own ideas and can put a lot of pressure on their discussion partner with a barrage of questions or suggestions.

As a former consultant myself, it was certainly one of my initial challenges not to take all the problem-solving responsibility in a coaching session. The use of pictures, metaphors and objects helped me to become less directive, less pushy. It quickly became clear that

I could not anticipate, predict, pre-cook or take ownership of these right-brain insights. Instead of working hard to ask the smartest question, suddenly it was much easier to explore an issue together as partners in the conversation. And with this attitude, the resulting insights were much more powerful for my clients, and they led to more action and change.

I wondered at the time if this was only true for me, helping me to let get of my own die-hard problem-solving habits. Teaching and supporting leaders and coaches for many years in using these tools has confirmed that the use of visual tools is equally powerful for others both in finding new information/insights and experiencing the 'we' in a coaching session.

Now that we know how to bring the right brain into our communication, we can focus on using its unique strengths, the topic of the next chapter.

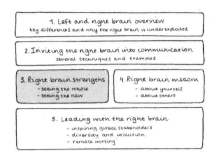

Accessing the right brain's unique strengths

'How are things going at the moment?'. Andrew and I are having our first coaching session, a virtual one. We met in person a few months earlier.

'Well, things are going rather well,' he says, 'certainly better than last year and I am really excited about my new responsibilities.'

Andrew has recently taken a new leadership role and is keen to establish himself as a strong leader in the business with a respected voice in the management team. Before our conversation, he emailed an overview of his role, his objectives for the coaching and topics for the conversation today. His email was thorough and quite unusually detailed for this early stage of our work together. I am curious how to interpret this action.

'If we look at it like this,' I say, while drawing a simple framework[22] on the Zoom whiteboard, 'where *doing good* is performance, making progress, etc. and feeling good is enjoyment, health, overall wellbeing. Where would you put yourself?'

Andrew puts a black dot more or less in the middle of the graph. 'And you mentioned things are better than last year, where were you then?' Andrew draws a second dot right in the left corner.

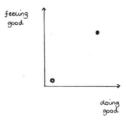

'Last year things were very difficult at work and I suffered a lot from that personally,' he explains, 'I am definitely better now but I want to grow my confidence as a leader, I want to really step into this new role.'.

'Ok,' I say, 'You emailed with some specific areas you want to work on. If that all goes well, where would you be on this graph then?' After a moment of reflection, Andrew draws a third dot:

He explains, 'I am feeling better now but I know that is largely due to things going better at work. I think that 'doing good' and 'feeling good' are much too connected for me. I worry that, with a set back at work, I will take a nose dive personally again. What I would like is to break this dependency between how I feel and how I am doing at work. There will always be ups and downs at work, our business has a lot of fluctuation, and if I get overly anxious and depressed when things are tough, it is bad for me personally and it is not good for the business either – as I am not at my best when it matters most. This last dot, that would be real progress for me.'.

For Andrew, a lot of things had happened in the last year. It would have been easy for us to spend an hour or more talking about everything that transpired, his challenges, what he did at the time, how others responded, what he liked about it and what he didn't.

You may recall a time where you casually asked someone, 'what's going on?' and you were bombarded by facts and details, and then more and more details, while you got that sinking feeling in your stomach and wished you'd never asked.

When we answer such a broad question, we can fall victim to this endless recounting of details. We might say, 'Well, let me tell you what is going on,' and then get entangled in a web of detail as each thing we say reminds us of something else. As a listener, in such an instance, our brain tries to add up what it hears to form a conclusion - is this good or bad? The brain is binary in that sense, it either wants to move towards (good) or get away from (bad).[23] When the conclusion is not quickly clear we get impatient as a listener as we want to know where this is going. Equally, as soon as we get a sense of the conclusion, we become impatient and want to move on. All in all, we humans tend not to be very patient listeners.

In contrast, when we ask someone a more direct question, 'how are you?' we can get a fast track to the conclusion, yet this often doesn't give us enough information. People tend to answer, 'great,' or, 'fine,' or, 'okay'. It sounds like a conclusion, yet unless we know someone very well, we don't know how to interpret these statements as we miss calibration. We then have the tendency to use our own frame of reference to calibrate which can easily lead to wrong assumptions. For example, for me, 'I'm fine' is a positive, but after twenty years in England, I know it often means something quite different.

In the conversation with Andrew, the calibration came from asking him where he had been and where he is aiming to get to, using the same visual and thus keeping the right brain in the lead. In the three dots he illustrated the past, the present and the aspiration for our work, and shared a lot of relevant context without having to share all the details.

Chapter One introduced the ability of the right brain to see the whole, the 'Gestalt' – synthesizing everything that is happening in a single overview. A typical leader's world is full of fragmentation, constantly divided attention, and non-stop communication over email, WhatsApp, Slack and other platforms. Being able to step back and, in a single glance, see the forest for the trees is a powerful right-brain skill. We have also discussed that anything new is experienced first in the right brain. In many instances, I have observed a close connection between these two right brains strengths of (i) seeing the whole and (ii) experiencing the new. After Andrew captured an overview of his situation with help of the framework, his new insight was that he wanted to break the dependency between results generated at work and his personal state of mind. This insight became an important guiding principle for our coaching work.

This chapter will cover a number of different techniques to access these two unique strengths of the right brain. The techniques are:

- Simple mechanisms to capture and calibrate the whole (like 'doing good, feeling good')
- Adding forces and direction
- Bringing a whole system to life

As you already know, the right brain needs a visual to communicate. One way to think about the different techniques in this chapter is giving the right brain a voice to share its strengths.

Simple mechanisms to capture and calibrate the whole

When getting an overall sense of what is going on at the start of a conversation, I distinguish two different approaches: sizing up an issue or sizing up the person.

Imagine someone introduces you to a challenge they are trying to resolve. This might be at the start of a conversation with a colleague who walks into your office looking for guidance or a friend in need of a listening ear.

To size up the issue, I am looking to understand how big this challenge is for the individual in question. A very effective way of doing so is to ask the person, 'show me with your hands (indicating the shape of a ball) how big this thing is'.

See the next page, take a moment, and make these gestures with your own hands; what do they imply for you?

A

B

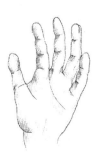

C

Often A means that the issue is relatively small, B means it is large but the person can still grab it, and C implies the issue is so large that it is difficult to hold. Another way to size up the issue is to ask someone 'on a scale of 0–10, how big of an issue is this?'. We have such a common implicit understanding of this scale that typically a topic sized A means 2–3; B means 5–6 and C means 9–10. Both techniques help to set context and calibrate issues in a quick and efficient manner. For example, between a leader and a team member when discussing project challenges; when identifying priorities in a feedback and development conversation; or when assessing topics during a due diligence, to name but a few.

The only caveat to be aware of is that some people deal with enormous challenges in their life which can impact how they relate to business problems. One of my clients had a child in hospital with a life-threatening condition and as a result there was no work problem higher than 'A' for them, even though some were rather substantial in the work context. For other people, a large challenge in their personal life can make a relatively minor work problem appear overwhelming. Thus, it is always good to follow up with a question that verifies our understanding, i.e. 'that seems to suggest you can grab it' or, 'how does this compare to some of the other challenges on your plate?'.

On another occasion, we might be more interested in getting a sense of how the person is doing themselves rather than with regards to a specific topic. For example, during a broader conversation with a team member about their work or their career, when you are concerned for someone's wellbeing, or if you are wondering whether a high performing team member is still enjoying their role. To size up the person, the 'doing good, feeling good' framework is very suitable.

Alternatively, another useful tool is the 'energy bucket'. Here you draw a bucket on a piece of paper or Zoom whiteboard and ask someone to draw their current energy level like a water level in the bucket.

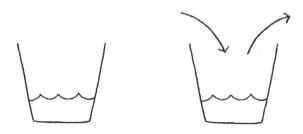

With a few simple questions you can calibrate the water level, e.g. 'How does that compare to your normal energy level, or a good energy level? How does your energy level fluctuate?'. You can then expand the conversation by drawing the arrows and asking what brings energy into the bucket, and what takes energy out. This overview often gives someone concrete ideas and actions to impact their energy level, and as a leader it can give you a clear indication of how you can best support them.

With these simple visuals people often are brutally honest. If they are not doing great, they will draw that energy level right at the bottom of the bucket or, as Andrew did, in the left bottom corner of the 'doing good, feeling good' graph.

It puzzled me for a while that visuals seem to aid this brutal honesty. Is the right side of the brain more honest than the left? I believe that, just as with the picture techniques we explored in Chapter Two, the visual provides some distance between the person and their experience and, with that distance, it is easier to acknowledge what is going on without feeling embarrassed or overwhelmed.

These techniques to size up the issue and/or the person can be a useful starting point for a conversation and quickly focus attention. However, when capturing the whole, the right brain is also able to share a lot more information.

Adding forces and directions

Alex has been successful in a sales role for many years, with a large client base in the financial sector. He is looking for a coach to support him in finding his next professional step as he feels he is not on the right path from a long term career perspective. He wants to change direction away from his current employer and role. After a few conversations, it appears that there is an obvious next step for him given his expertise, namely, to find a role in private banking. And yet, while it logically all fits together, Alex doesn't seem very enthusiastic about this option, and is not taking much action in that direction.

 When someone is not being pro-active, it is often because there are forces at play that are not yet known, either to the individual themselves or to anyone else. This is where the right brain comes in. Using the right brain we are able to see and to highlight such forces, like visualizing a force field. For this purpose, I often carry around post-its, and my favourites are the arrow shaped ones.

To get started, Alex lists the different factors that would influence his career choice, and writes each factor on a separate post-it:

- personal learning path / acquiring new skills
- future career opportunities / money-earning potential
- using current client base in a new role
- global brand & reach of future employer

- location/quality of life (where to live, proximity to friends and family, sports etc.)
- work environment (boss, colleague, politics)
- building on key strengths in people skills (i.e. sales)

Our next step is to create an image of these factors and the force they generate with regard to Alex's career options. Sitting at a square table, I point to the side of the table opposite Alex and say 'let's say that is the direction of the private banking option. Which factors are pointing in that direction?'. He quickly puts down the first two post-it notes. 'And how about the others...?'

One by one he takes the other post-its and put them down on the table in different directions. At this point, I am deliberately not saying much in order to keep him working from his right brain without any left-brain analysis kicking in. I don't want him to think too much about it, just to put the post-its down.

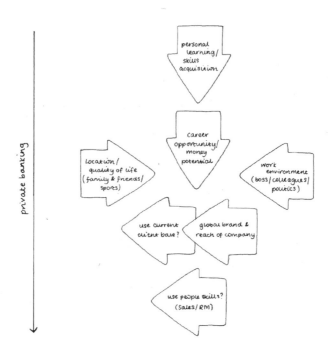

We look at the image together.

'What are you seeing?' I ask.

His first remark is that so few of the post-its are pointing into the direction of private banking. He then notices how there is a cluster of others pointing together in a different direction: work environment / brand / client base/ people skills. He doesn't know exactly what they are pointing towards, so we focus on the fact that these factors are a movement together, driving to a different direction.

He next reflects that this image illustrates his feeling that the private bank option is not going to put him on a path that truly energizes him. He is intrigued that the other factors are aligned into one directional force and confirms that this feels right.

His second observation is that the 'location/ quality of life' post-it is seemingly going against everything. Location had featured greatly in several of our previous conversations. He is currently living in London and there is a strong desire in him to stay there. At the same time, he does not see himself in London long term. Seeing this opposing force in front of him, made it clear the location factor causes him to be quite stuck. We discuss that he is making a lot of assumptions about location / quality of life that are influencing which options he even looks at. Perhaps it would be possible to park this consideration for a little while as he is gathering more information. He agrees and our conversation refocuses on exploring what the cluster of other factors might be pointing towards.

Zooming in on the factor 'global brand and reach of company', I wonder aloud what kind of organizations excite him. He immediately talks about the new tech giants such as Google, Amazon, Microsoft. How could his client base and expertise be valuable for such organizations? Slowly the idea of selling software solutions in the financial sector starts to shape up. Alex decides, as a result of this exercise, to explore opportunities with the new tech giants.

His network doesn't naturally extend into these companies, so he needs to be creative, persistent, and patient. Finally, his efforts and patience pay off and he has now been working for one of the tech giants for several years. He was able to make a flying start using his expertise of selling in the financial sector and today covers an array of other sectors as well. He has moved away from the UK to the continent and has built a very good life around sports, friends, and family.

With the post-its, the relevant factors influencing his career choice and the relationships between them became clear to Alex. In other words, he saw his career decision 'system' mapped out in front of him.

Bringing the whole system to life

System Dynamics, developed by Jay W. Forrester[24] in the 1950s at the MIT Sloan School of Management models the relationships between all the parts of a system and how those relationships influence the behavior of the system over time[25]. As a student at MIT Sloan in my twenties, the course 'Introduction to System Dynamics' opened my eyes to the interconnections between concrete and 'soft' factors in a system, the visible and invisible, the quantifiable and qualitative. When the system doesn't produce an expected outcome, it means there are interrelationships not yet understood and included.

Also in the 1950s, Murray Bowen started his career as a psychologist and proceeded to develop the 'Family Systems Theory'.[26] He defined the family as a complex social system and argued for looking at the system as a whole to understand dynamics between family members. Bert Hellinger, a few decades later, developed an approach that he called 'Family Constellations' to look into patterns of behavior, visible and hidden, between family members.[27] A 'constellation' is defined as a three-dimensional spatial model of a relationship system. In a family constellation, individuals are positioned in a room as stand-ins for family members, a unique way of visualizing a system. By doing so, people can find new paths to move beyond decades of family conflict. Today this is a well-accepted therapy approach that provides deep healing in a way that defies logic.

When the right brain gives a visual representation of the system, an understanding of 'what is' without delving into all the history of how the system was formed, it frees up the mind and energy for exploring new perspectives and ideas. This is how I see the connection between the right brain's strengths of seeing the whole and experiencing the new.

I will illustrate two examples below in bringing systems to life, one that is easy to apply in regular business conversations, and one that is more suited to a coaching session.

'The team is just not working,' is how Rose starts our conversation. 'I have been trying to bring more collaboration in how we work together, and we have done some socializing to get to know each other, yet I see little progress.'

'Are you up for looking at this in a creative way?' I propose. She agrees and, taking a piece of paper from the flipchart in the meeting room and grabbing a few markers, I ask her to draw the team.

Rose shows her surprise and says, ' I can't really draw'.

'No worries, me neither, this can be really simple,' I say, while handing her the paper and the markers. She draws the following picture:

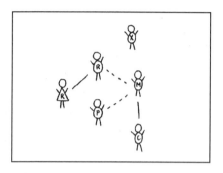

Earlier, when Rose arrived, she had taken a seat opposite me at the conference table as people so often do. While handing her the paper and pens, I take the opportunity to sit next to her so we can look at the drawing together, supporting the right brain experience of 'we'.

When she stops drawing, I ask her what she sees.

'It looks disjointed,' she replies, 'and some of the distances quite large. This is what it feels like when we work together, as if we are just too far apart.'.

'I see that too, and what else strikes you?'

'I am one of people that is on the outside, I am not in the hub of the team. Also, C and X are not in the core of the team.'

After a bit more talking, I say, 'I also keep noticing that no-one has a facial expression.'.

Rose reflects that she doesn't really know how everyone is feeling – she recently asked them; everyone said they were okay, and yet it had felt disingenuous to her at the time.

'What would you guess about their feelings?' Rose draws the following:

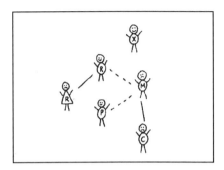

After a moment she says, 'I have a major issue with M – he is not performing well and I haven't addressed it, it's poisoning the collaboration in the whole team and C is very affected. Also my connection with P is too weak. I have felt out of my depth in discussions with him and have not done enough 1:1s.'.

After asking her if there was anything else she notices, and not having further things that seem immediately relevant to me, I ask, 'So what would make this better?'. Rose immediately starts talking and I quickly hand her back the pens with, 'can you draw that?'.

She proceeds, 'So this needs to be the new core team, and it can only work if I build the connection between myself and P, and address

the performance issues of M. It would be great if you could help me make a plan of how to do that.'.

We finish by discussing next steps she can take to address both those issues. For example, for M we specify the feedback she needs to give and for P she identifies a key piece of work that they can do together, as well as opportunities to see each other in person more regularly. None of these steps are revolutionary in themselves; it is rather the intention behind them that gives Rose what she needs to act.

In this example, drawing the current team system provides us with an immediate shared understanding of the situation. Even though Rose's picture is simple and it takes only a few moments to draw, there is a lot to observe:

- What are the first things she draws?
- What is her energy while drawing (strong strokes vs light strokes)?
- Is there white space on the paper?
- Where does she put herself?
- Are there facial expressions?

When I work with leaders on how to apply coaching skills in their context, and we practice with drawing, they often remark on how much there is to observe. One of them once said, 'It's like finding new dimensions of information, and then observing in these multiple dimensions at once. Surprisingly, this is easier than I thought it would be.' It so happens that we have more than enough bandwidth to expand our observations. Our brains can process words much faster than someone can speak them, yet another reason why we can quickly get distracted when listening. So if we use our processing power to observe relevant information on multiple dimensions, we can avoid getting distracted.

When drawing, there is often so much information within the space of a few minutes that it is perhaps most important to take it slowly. Build the conversation around a handful of observations and don't try to bring in too much. Trust the right brain of the other person to show what's most relevant, and trust your own right brain to pick up the key signals. One key thing to remember is that, in a system, position or place is considered significant and holds a lot of information. So, where objects or people are on the page, in absolute and relative terms, holds meaning. For example, Rose's positioning of herself outside the hub of the team.

A few practical pointers for the first step in a drawing process:

- Ask the person who draws to reflect on their picture first, and acknowledge what they see.
- Ask 'what else?' once or twice, to probe their reflections, before adding any of your own observations.
- Say something about the drawing to emphasize that you are looking at it together, that you are noticing things about the picture and that you are adding your resources to the process.
- Avoid questions that start digging into the past like 'how long have you been working together?' or that start looking for explanations such as 'why do you think you don't know how they feel?'

After the initial drawing of the current situation, the next step is to see what forces would improve the system. Simple questions are essential such as, 'what would make this better?' or, 'where do you want this to go?' or, 'what movement would help the situation?'. Give the person the pen immediately so you get the input on the picture. Without that, the discussion will slip into left-brain problem solving and the right brain's input might be missed. What Rose did was to increase the lines between her and the key team members. She drew the thicker lines with a burst of energy, rapidly going back and forth multiple times. When we discussed what this movement represented, she identified the need for increased interactions driven by her with more energy, spontaneity, purpose – to initiate stronger bonds between the team members. Then, we brainstormed what actions she could take to realize this.

It may sound somewhat magical, but the answers are always on the paper, even if it takes time to see them. Just last week, I was showing this technique to a group of coaches in training while doing a demo session with one of the participants. In the second step of the process, looking at how the situation could be made better, he drew one line that held all the answers to a situation that was emotionally highly challenging. It happened so fast that it took both of us some time to see the line and to realize what it implied. When working in this way, I often have to make a real effort to stop my own problem-solving engine kicking in, it is an impatient beast and it can literally feel like I have to hold it back by the reins. Patience, attention and curiosity for what happens on the paper are the qualities we need to listen to the right brain's input.

The next example is for those of you who would like to take this way of working to the next level in your capacity as an internal or external coach. Instead of drawing, the process uses wooden figures to create a system as a 'constellation' and builds on the principles of systemic coaching. In his excellent book 'Systemic Coaching and Constellations',[28] John Whittington details this approach and illustrates how to use it with individuals and teams. Next to wooden figures, other good constellation objects are stones or marbles – anything that enables the coachee to move an object, change its position, and experiment what feels right or wrong spatially. This adds an additional dimension beyond a drawing.

Lia is interested to explore the dynamics in the leadership team that she has recently joined. She has observed different groupings in the team and is wondering how she can best contribute to the team.

To get started, I ask Lia if she can illustrate the team set up with the wooden figures. She puts the figures together in the following way:

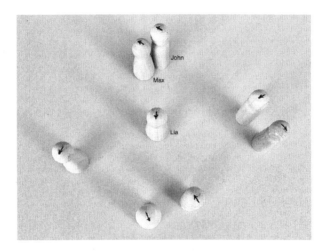

'What do you notice?' I ask her. Lia replies, 'A few things. First my boss (Max) and his boss above him (John) are glued together and that doesn't look right. Also, putting myself in the middle of the team doesn't feel right either.'.

'And what about the arrows?'

When asking Lia to set up the team, I made no mention of the arrows on the top of each figure. The arrows on the wooden figures were added to give directional force to the constellation and the right brain instinctively takes such data into consideration.

'I hadn't noticed them,' Lia said, 'what do they mean?'.

'It depends, sometimes they have something to do with the direction that someone is heading. What could they mean here?'

Lia ponders on this question for a moment as she frequently does in our conversations. While some people slip into left-brain detailing or problem solving, I already know that Lia keeps using her right brain and stays with the image. 'Well,' she says, 'the arrows indicate alignment, they show whether team members are working in the same direction or actually not really collaborating at all. I am in the middle twirling around trying to align with different team members.'.

We talk a while longer about the current situation and, when nothing else significant appears, we move to the next key question: 'What would be good for the dynamics in the team?'.

'First,' Lia says, 'John needs to back off. As long as he and Max are glued together, Max is not really leading the team and which in turn also confuses my role.'.

'What would be a better position for John to move to?'

Lia picks up the figure representing John and experiments with a few positions. 'Here feels right,' she concludes. We explore what that distance would represent in reality. Lia identifies a few practical things such as meetings John should not attend, emails Max should send rather than John, etc.

We then look at the figures again to see what else would be good for the dynamics of the team. Lia reflects that the different groupings of team members make sense given their geographical focus as the groupings loosely represent regions. She identifies that the next step would be to create more directional alignment within the regions as well as between the regions and Max. This is more important than complete alignment between regions. For this to happen, she says, Max and I need to first focus on the team members within each of the regions with whom we have most contact, and leverage their influence to get alignment within. Secondly, Max needs to build stronger relationships with each region himself, he should not rely so heavily on the relationships that John or I have built. I need to support Max to do this.

Finally, we move to Lia's place in the image – from what position would she be able to best support Max and the team? She places herself less in the middle and much closer to Max, aligning with his direction.

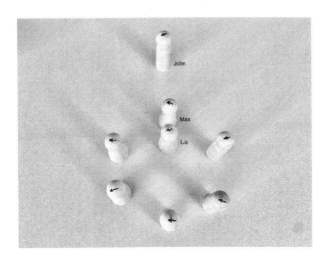

This conversation took place over four years ago. To refresh my own memory, I reconnected with Lia and, to my surprise, she immediately re-created the team configuration. 'I still remember it exactly,' she said.

It was not the first time that someone could easily recall a visual memory from a conversation we had years ago. You have likely experienced it yourself for instance when you are trying to remember what was said during a meeting and you can't recall the precise discussion, but you can picture which slide was showing at that time, or who was sitting where.

An old Chinese proverb famously states, 'I hear and I forget, I see and I remember, I do and I understand'. There is now a name for this phenomenon, it's called the *'picture superiority effect'*. While it has been demonstrated in numerous ways, the explanations are still subject to debate. In the early 1970s, Allan Paivio hypothesized a dual-coding theory, suggesting that our brains dually encode images but encode words only once.[29]

Memory is complex and is a large field of scientific study. Alongside the visual sense, our other senses also play a big role in our memory. When I smell Assam tea, I am sitting in my grandmother's living room. Certain Lily Allen songs transport me back to a jeep in Namibia, one of our best family road trips. The body also plays a big role in memory and we will explore this more in the next chapter.

What matters to me in a business coaching context is to make use of such different kinds of memory to support someone's development process. Lia's image of being positioned next to her boss Max in wooden figures, rather than being in the middle of the team, guided her behaviors in a way that complemented her concrete action plans. Sandy, in the previous chapter, printed out the picture that described how she wanted to be in her new project and framed it on her desk. In both these examples, the right brain's visual provided a guide for the future, a powerful reminder to embrace a role. Often, it is not possible to foresee all the possible situations one might encounter but the image can help to keep you focussed on what is important, and to guide you through.

Flow of a coaching session with right brain strengths

The following flow is especially useful when a coachee introduces a topic that involves a complex dynamic, within their own life, within a team, or within any other constellation of people.

- Start by identifying the topic of the conversation. It is not necessary to identify the required outcome in precise terms.

- Ask for permission to explore this topic in a more creative way. You can mention that it is especially useful to understand the dynamics at play. Such an explanation can help the left brain to relax into the discussion. Another helpful thing to add is that you will do some exploration together and then analyze it to identify useful next steps.

- With your first question, your aim is to identify relevant parts of the system and map the system. Sometimes this happens in one step, sometimes in two. For example, when you are looking into a team dynamic, you can ask someone to draw the team, or, when using objects, you can ask to show what the team looks like now (one step). When you are looking for relevant forces or factors at play, it often works best to list them first and then map them – as in the Alex example with the post-it notes (two steps).

- Find a way to sit so you can easily look at the system together.

- Once the system is mapped out, take time to explore what's on the table. As with the pictures, always ask your coachee first for their observations. Sometimes they immediately want to analyze what something means. However, it is essential not to do so and instead to take time gathering more observations. Typically, the best way to do this is to acknowledge their thoughts, say that you will definitely explore that further in a bit, and immediately ask what else they notice. Do not tell them that they aren't allowed to analyze it now as it will most likely completely disrupt the process.

- It is essential to offer some of your own observations early in the conversation; your coachee will likely feel self-conscious doing this creative process and, unless you participate, they will feel too exposed.

- Your observations have to be about the system in front of you, or about something you observed in how your coachee put the system together. And remember to observe rather than question. For example: 'These two team members are far apart compared to the others.' Not, 'Why are these two so far apart?'.

- The next step is to explore what would improve the situation/ team dynamic. You can ask this question very broadly. At this point most coachees start talking but you need to guide them quickly (gently and firmly) to show it on the system they have already mapped. 'What would that look like...?'

- Use the last part of the session, to make sense of the input, and broadly investigate next steps together.

Accessing the right brain's unique strengths
– the key concepts

This chapter focussed on how to use two unique strengths of the right brain: seeing the whole and seeing the new. Because the right brain experiences the entirety of the present moment, it can convey all the richness of that moment in a single visual. We don't get information about the past, such as how or why a situation was created, but we see what the reality is right now.

We can access this strength at a high level, like observing something from distance, and this gives us an appreciation of how big, serious or challenging an issue is. This technique is referred to as sizing up the issue or sizing up the person.

In addition, the right brain can also give us an image of the dynamics of a situation, like visualizing a forcefield or describing a system in action. This is particularly useful to understand dynamics between people or within a person.

Often, the two right brain strengths combine naturally in the same discussion by (i) understanding the current situation and (ii) exploring what would improve it. The key principles are:

- Ask short open questions; trust the right brain to highlight what is relevant.
- Observe on different levels. Observe what somebody draws, for example, but also what they draw first, what they draw with more energy, when they hesitate, etc.
- Keep it simple. There is more likely to be too much information than not enough. Again, trust the right brain to direct the attention of the conversation.

- Bring patience, attention and curiosity rather than active problem solving.
- Explore together.

There always needs to be a balance between involving the right brain and the left brain in a discussion. A conversation is never just a right-brain conversation. In an ideal scenario, the left brain participates actively at the start with setting a good outcome for the discussion and sharing some pertinent facts, without getting lost in detail. Then you invite the right brain to participate and use its strengths. And towards the end you steer back towards left-brain qualities to identify tangible next steps and clarify priorities. This feels like a conversation which is both rich and complete.

Occasionally, at the end of a right-brain-driven conversation, there isn't enough time to discuss concrete actions, or it might not seem like the appropriate thing to do. Right-brain processing tends to linger and produce additional insights well beyond the working session. As we are used to immediately identifying actions and accountabilities, this can feel a bit too open-ended. In a coaching program, with regular meetings, I will always ask my coachee at the start of a conversation what other reflections they had since our last meeting, especially when we had a predominantly right-brain discussion. In a day-to-day business setting, it can also be a good practice to do a check in within a day or two and ask someone to confirm which actions they are taking.

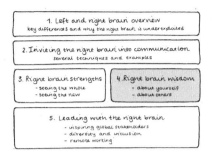

Tapping into the wisdom of the right brain

'How do you feel?'

When I started coaching, I noticed that asking someone, 'How do you feel?' usually did not generate much discussion. Responses were often as basic as 'fine' or 'okay', similar to when asked 'How are you?' as discussed earlier. Sometimes asking about feelings even stalled a conversation. When learning to coach, we were encouraged to focus on the person as well as the issues so when my attempts to ask about feelings were unproductive, I was rather puzzled.

Then I noticed that if instead I asked, 'How are you experiencing this [situation]?', the responses changed. Answers were much richer such as, 'This is a really mixed experience for me, I am annoyed because…, but at the same time excited because…, and somewhat surprised that…'. Although I didn't directly ask people about feelings, their responses revealed much more about how they felt and often naturally described different aspects of their experience.

Questions such as, 'How is this affecting you?', or even, simply, 'What is it like for you?', had the same effect. Over time, I learned to avoid asking directly about feelings, but remained puzzled about why the direct question, 'How do you feel?' didn't work – we all have feelings, don't we?

Chapter One introduced the intricate connections between the body, the brain and our emotions and the fact that information from the whole of the body enters the right brain first. When we are asking someone to describe a feeling we are asking them for the outcome of a highly complex process, triggering a response from the left brain which tries to express an accurate, succinct answer to the question. Yet, we seldom have just one feeling at any given time – typically, we have a lot of feelings simultaneously and this is easier for the right brain to process than for the left brain.

It is said that the right side of the brain has an *'and'* stance, taking in everything from a single moment simultaneously, and seeing a world full of connections, while the left side of the brain, logical, linear, structured, takes the *'or'* stance.[30] The right brain, with its *'and'* stance, can digest the existence of several feelings at the same time, even if they seem contradictory. We can be excited and annoyed and relaxed. When we ask, 'How are you feeling?', we are asking the left side of our brain to verbalize something that, in many cases, it cannot truly answer.

So what happens when we change the question to, 'What do you experience?', and why does that lead to such a different response? The verb 'experience' means to 'participate in or undergo', or 'to be aesthetically or emotionally moved by – to feel - something that happens to us'.[31] It presupposes that what happens to us can be described. This subtly puts the 'experiencer' in the position of the observer – observing their responses to a situation, thereby paving the way to give a narrative of the event, with all its twists and turns and complexity of emotion, rather than a conclusion. In a narrative, or story, contrasting elements are interesting rather than problematic, otherwise the story would be boring. In addition to the first richer response to 'What do you experience?' I also found that with a little bit of probing such as, 'And what else was going on for you?', more feelings were shared – often deeper and more detailed still.

Something similar happens when inquiring about other people's feelings. A question such as, 'How are your team members feeling at the moment?', often results in another basic response (okay/bad/not sure) but asking someone, 'How is the team experiencing this?', generates the much richer response.

This chapter focuses on the connection between the right brain, our emotional and social lives, and our body. Through this connection, the right brain is a source of knowledge and information for us and about us, and we will explore how to make use of this wisdom. This, more than anything we have explored so far, requires an interplay between our hemispheres, making the most out of the unique qualities of both the right and the left side of the brain. The chapter will guide you through the following topics:

- Understanding the brain-body-emotion connection
- Appreciating the knowledge of the right brain
- Tapping into the wisdom of the right-brain

Before diving in, let's take a look at a few other simple sentences that we use frequently in conversations, and review how they trigger the hemispheres.

'What do you think?'

Most likely you have asked and been asked this question many times today. It is almost the standard way we proceed after a topic has been introduced in a discussion. Knowing what you know now about the two hemispheres, it probably doesn't come as a surprise that this question – for most people – generates a left-brain-dominant response: a logical, structured, argument. The Oxford Dictionary even defines a thinking person as 'someone using thorough or rational judgment'. The question, 'What do you think?' typically invites a conclusion or an opinion, rather than a description.

Once an opinion has been stated, many people naturally focus on proving or defending their opinion rather than investigating it.

Imagine the following discussion between an executive (let's call him Tom) and one of his direct reports (Sean), when discussing the roll-out of a new initiative:

Tom: 'What do you think about the buy-in for the initiative?'

Sean: 'I think overall the team is on board.'

Tom: 'Great, why do you think so?'

Sean: 'Well, I see team members actively participating in the discussions, with a lot of energy and interest.'

Tom: 'Are you sure? It is important at this stage to make sure we get the right buy-in.'

Sean: ' Yes, I was pleasantly surprised by their engagement, let me share some of the questions that came up...'

People get easily entrenched in their position. When that happens, retracing the facts and assumptions that have shaped an opinion can be time consuming. In addition, if someone knows any facts that challenge their opinion, they are usually not freely offered.

With a small adjustment in words, we can avoid this trap:

Tom: 'What do you think about the buy-in of the initiative?'

Sean: 'I think overall the team is on board.'

Tom: 'Great, what are you <u>seeing</u>?'

Sean: 'Well, I see many team members actively participating in the discussions, with a lot of energy and interest. Some, I can see, are rather quiet and not very engaged. These are usually the quiet people in the group, so I am not too bothered by that.'

Tom: 'Ok, that sound promising indeed. <u>Anything else you see?</u>'

Sean: 'Now that I am playing back the discussions in my mind, there is just one of the normally vocal people who was not engaging on this topic. Overall, I still have the impression the team is on board, but I do wonder what his view is as he is a key influencer in the team.'

Tom: 'Ok, can you find out some more? Sometimes teams are less committed than they show, and it can present us with complications at a later stage.'

Sean: 'I'll speak to him today and see what I learn. I'll keep you posted.'

Facts are observed through our senses, and questions such as, 'What do you see?' or, 'What do you hear?' tend to lead to a recounting of those facts, rather than the interpretation of the facts. The other senses – smell, taste, touch – also generate interesting input, each with their own twist. 'How does this smell/taste?' tends to tap into our intuition, our gut feel. 'How is this touching you?', activating our sense of touch, stimulates a response similar to, 'How is this affecting you?'.

Each of the five senses brings its own richness to a conversation. By invoking the senses, we bring in body information which invites right-brain participation. The right brain's *'and'* ability generates a wealth of information as input to our logical, rational, problem-solving abilities and is a fruitful way to involve the unique skills of both hemispheres.

In your next conversations, do some experimenting with invoking the senses in your questions or asking how someone is experiencing a challenging situation, and *see* what happens.

'Where do you stand?'

In my native language Dutch, a different and often-asked question is, 'Hoe sta jij erin?' best translated as, 'Where do you stand?'. At first glance a rather odd thing to say as it infers that our body has a position towards a topic. I assume you don't often ask yourself how your body is positioned towards the new company initiative, health care funding or global warming. It is tempting to dismiss such a phrase as just something we say without placing too much literal meaning on it. And yet there are quite a few expressions in common use referencing posture – lining up the parties, positioning topics or stepping into someone's shoes.

In the last chapter we saw that, for a system, position is highly significant, that it holds a lot of relevant information. In one of our workshops, we use positioning to help leaders think about where they are in terms of their leadership ambition. We invite participants to stand on one side of the room and offer them a coloured A4 card as a token of their ambition.

We ask them to put the card somewhere on the floor in the room, representing how far away that ambition is for them. Participants will put the cards in different places – some right in front of them, some all the way across the room and others somewhere in between. We ask them to look at their ambition and experience the forces that pull them towards the aspiration, and the forces that hold them in place, even swaying their bodies slightly forward and backwards to notice the forces. Then, we ask them to slowly take one step forward. What is it is like to stand in this new place and what is happening to the forces? Which forces are pulling them forward, and which are holding them back?

We then ask them to go and stand in the place where they would like to be in the room. Some participants take another step forward, others move all the way forward to stand on their coloured card. From this next place, we ask them to turn around and look back at where they came from and, in their minds eye, see themselves standing in their original spot. What advice would they give themselves?

After this experience, we suggest they sit down, take some notes of their observations and then write down what actions they want to take. With this last step, we invite the left brain to actively participate, process the experience and look ahead to identify actions. We finish by asking participants to share something about their experience and the first action they will take.

Some participants have an insightful experience that they can articulate, for example, 'At first, my ambition felt far away. I want to move towards P&L[32] responsibility, become a business leader. But then, when I took the first step, I wanted to keep moving forward – I felt such a strong pull and I realized it doesn't matter what my first step is, it can be anything. So what I am going to do tomorrow is.....'.

Other participants have an experience that they can't immediately grasp such as, 'I didn't want to move towards my ambition, I felt resistance and something strong holding me in place – I am not fully sure what that was about.'. And there are always some who admit they didn't experience anything particularly insightful while standing in the room.

How can we make sense of these experiences? What exactly is this information coming from the body – where does it come from and can it be trusted? And why do some people get much more input than others – while stepping towards some colourful cards representing their ambitions?

We will dive into the brain-body-emotion connection in more depth to explore these questions.

Understanding the brain-body-emotion connection

Chapter One introduced the concept that emotions correspond with physical sensations in our body. When our heart races - we feel anxious, or maybe excited; when our face is soft and our mouth turns upwards - we feel happy; when our gut is churning – we are scared. Through our mirror neurons we can have physical sensations that replicate what someone else is experiencing. This is how we can relate to the emotions of others. As information from the whole body enters the right brain first, the right brain often has knowledge, a wisdom, about our own experiences and the experiences of others, that the left brain does not have.

As Daniel Siegel expertly lays out in his wonderful book 'Mindsight',[33] when we are babies, we can only express non-verbally and we do so using our bodies with crying, frowning, moving our arms and legs, smiling, snuggling, and more. When our caregivers respond appropriately and predictably to our non-verbal signals, we feel safe and connected to them. This exchange segments the connection between our body and how we feel. These non-verbal signals are created and perceived by the right side of the brain, which is more developed during the first years of our life. When words become more important after these early years, the left brain becomes more active.

Throughout any normal childhood or adolescence, when situations create emotions that are too raw and overwhelming, the brain protects us by reducing awareness of the corresponding body signals. The brain learns to focus attention elsewhere, for example on conceptual problems, future plans or past events. By doing so, we pay less attention to the body and thereby reduce the intensity of the present moment. In some cases, when someone experiences trauma, the connection between the body and the right brain can be significantly reduced as a survival mechanism. This is the aforementioned door between our right brain and our body.

Even without trauma or overwhelming emotional experiences, the western educational system is not tailored to explore the body-brain connection in our formative learning years. In a business context, many of my coachees – well-functioning, healthy adults – find it hard to notice physical sensations and information from their body, other than aches and pains. They are simply not used to tuning into this kind of data.

The good news is that we can continue to develop the ability to understand body information well into our old age. We can re-train our brain to be more aware of, and pay more attention to, our body. If you are or have been an athlete at some point in your life, you may have learned to pay attention to your body as part of your training, so that you notice areas of tension to avoid injuries. Yoga and Tai Chi involve a high level of body relaxation which can increase body awareness. Another practical and easily accessible way to acquire greater body awareness is through mindfulness practices called body scans. With the help of a recording, you learn to pay attention to different parts of your body. There are many apps, such as Headspace,[34] offering practices. For a small taster, see the grey box below:

Starting with body awareness (3 min exercise)

Once you have read the instructions below, sit in a chair with your feet flat on the floor, back straight, hands in your lap, shoulders back and relaxed (hanging down), chin tucked in slightly.

Close your eyes or lower your gaze to do the exercise.

Imagine a camera moving through your body, observing without judgement your physical sensations. The camera notices what parts are tight, what parts are relaxed, what parts are restless, hot, cold, etc. Some parts you might notice more than others, the camera notices them too but it doesn't try to change anything, it only observes.

Let the camera start in the toes in your left foot, travel up your left leg, up the spine, explore the left arm and shoulder move up the neck over your head and face, explore the right shoulder and arm, travel down past the heart, through the lungs and then your internal organs and finally down the right leg, ending in the toes of your right foot.

If you get distracted and lose track of the camera, smile, and pick it up again from where you last remember.

Enjoy it, wiggle your left toes and let the camera begin its journey.

When finished, ask yourself what you noticed and what you are curious to check out on your next camera tour.

A word of caution. When someone's experience of their body information and/or their emotions is limited and doesn't grow once they pay more attention, it is often because their brain has evolved to keep this door closed for a good reason. It is not the responsibility of coaches, colleagues or friends to try to push this door further open. This has to be the choice of the individual, as much as it is their choice to seek the guidance that works for them.

Appreciating the knowledge of the right brain

Beyond emotions, our bodies are able to express a lot more to us. Here is a simple example that you may recognize. A few weeks ago, I was leaving the house and, as I stepped through the door, my body hesitated. I paused, looked around me, and saw my phone still lying on the table. My body conveyed a message that had the potential to impact my day.

To fully appreciate the richness of body information, it is essential to understand that there is a two-way exchange between your brain and your body. Your body doesn't just produce information that we are trying to get our brain to listen to, our brain influences and constantly primes the body for what it experiences.

An example. There is, scientists have discovered, much higher traffic from our brain to our eyes than from our eyes to our brain.[35] The brain predicts what our eyes will see and that constitutes most of the traffic. The traffic from our eyes to the brain is mostly the difference to the prediction. I experienced this recently. Our youngest daughter changed her hair colour, from dark brown to ginger. For the first two days it was like she had an orange beacon around her head, it startled me every time I saw her. After two days, this vivid appearance of her hair in my field of vision was gone. My brain had adjusted the prediction.

Our brain doesn't only predict our field of vision, it predicts everything that we perceive through our five senses, what we will hear, what we will touch, what we will taste or smell. Our brain also predicts what our body needs moment to moment, how fast our heart needs to beat or what our hormonal balance needs to be. In the same way, the brain predicts our emotional experience and, in doing so, creates the physical experience of emotions in our body. So now we have a twist in the plot: how can we trust our body information if it is constructed by our own brain's predictions?

Let's take a step back. We all know that our thoughts have a big impact on our experience of the world. As is often said, 'perception is reality'. If you believe your colleague is annoying, you will pay attention to the things they do that annoy you even if that is only a small percentage of their actions. You probably won't even notice most of their other actions. Our brain is highly selective and only brings information into our conscious awareness that it deems relevant. When you decide you like the new Jaguar E-PACE, for the following few days you will see that car everywhere. Of course, those cars have not suddenly appeared, they were there all along but the data didn't enter your consciousness. The left brain's model of reality is a big driver of this selectiveness, and predicts what we observe.

Indeed, our body information is also based on the brain's own predictions, yet we access a source of information that is beyond the left-brain model of reality and thus we can bring new information into our conscious awareness. These predictions are based on an enormous amount of data that is essential to who we are, including our life experiences, our environment (including what our mirror neurons generate), our personality, our hopes and dreams, and our genetic make-up. There are examples of firefighters walking out of buildings seconds before they collapse.[36] They don't know what specifically made them leave the building at that moment, they just knew to listen when their body said, 'Let's go'. Call it instinct, call it gutfeel – it originates in our bodies.

So, how is this all relevant to the exercise on leadership ambitions described earlier? When we are considering our ambitions, our brain is consumed with predictions – how we want to grow, where we want to be – and takes into account all the factors that impact our ambition, those we are conscious of as well as those that live in our unconscious. In the exercise, we are asking the body to communicate these predictions, and express all this information in a tangible way. The right brain plays a critical role in this process as it is able to capture the whole, and is strongly connected to body information . This is what I call tapping into the wisdom of the right brain.

In an entertaining TED Talk, *'The psychology of your future self'*, Dan Gilbert makes a convincing argument that we, in every decade of our life, change more than we expect to change.[37] He states:

'Human beings are works in progress that mistakenly think they are finished.'

It seems to me he illustrates beautifully that a big part of us, half of our brain in fact, believes it has full clarity, about the past, present and future – and that this is an illusion.

Nevertheless, to make use of the wisdom of our right brain, the left brain has an essential role to play. Getting back to the earlier example of hesitating in the doorway, once I notice my body hesitating, my left brain steps in and analyzes the situation. It quickly deduces that I have probably forgotten something as this has happened before. Instantly a list of essential items pops up in my mind: keys, computer, wallet, glasses, phone… Eureka! My phone enters the visual field. I pick it up and off I go.

Interestingly, a few days later exactly the same thing happens at the doorway but even though I pause, following my body's hesitation, I can't figure out what I have forgotten. There is nothing missing in my list of essential items and my mind chatter immediately shifts to suggest I should not waste any more time – I am already late, it is probably nothing, I should leave. About thirty minutes later, I realize what I have forgotten: a pre-packed bag which I had even put in the hallway, but it was such an unusual item to bring along that I didn't see it (meaning it wasn't selected as relevant) when looking around.

Interpreting body information requires an immediate interplay between the left and the right side of the brain. As we know the left brain tends to dismiss right brain input, hence this needs some finessing. The left brain initially needs to 'relax' so new information arriving through the right brain can be brought into awareness and acknowledged, after which the left brain can analyze the new information to make it tangible. The new information needs to be found relevant, otherwise we move on. Not surprising, as spending one hour in the doorway trying to figure out what you missed is not very practical. Especially as the body information could, after all, just be the result of a groaning stomach following a heavy breakfast.

Tapping into the wisdom of the right brain

The wisdom of the right brain can be explored on a few different levels. Firstly, we will look at what we can do on a personal level to learn about ourselves through our body information. Secondly, we will look at applications on a team level. Lastly, we'll look more broadly at applying right-brain wisdom in our relationships with others.

Tapping into the wisdom of the right brain on a personal level

As illustrated by the doorway example, when our body hesitates it is wise to pause, pay attention and see if you can make sense of the information. With practice, and attention, we can become better at this, both in noticing the body hesitating and in figuring out what it means. How else can we tap into the right brain in our everyday lives?

We are often mentally, emotionally, and physically stuck at the same time and, in most everyday situations, it is quicker to get out of this deadlock by moving our bodies than by moving our minds. Getting out of our chairs, stretching, getting a glass of water – simple body movements can have a positive impact on our brain. You probably do a lot of that already without realizing, though you may be telling yourself you are wasting time. In team meetings, people get up and walk around and coffee breaks are called when the discussion stalls.

There is a fine line between allowing yourself to get distracted and listening to your body signals, but also here, when we pay attention, we can notice the difference. In any meeting, virtual or in-person, stretching or moving around for a minute can breathe fresh air into the discussion and lead to new ideas. When you are the leader in the room, you are best placed to initiate such a practice, especially so in a virtual setting where it is less natural to get up.

In general, it is often quicker to notice what our body is doing than what is happening to our thoughts or emotions. For example, when I am feeling bored and mentally disengaged in a conversation, I tend to lean backwards rather than forward. I realized years ago that I could catch myself before I had become fully switched off by noticing when I started leaning backwards. My body was showing what was happening before I was consciously aware of it. Even more interesting, I found I was able to reverse this process – by leaning forward again I re-engaged. In other words, through our body, we can directly influence how we show up by taking the following steps:

- Observe our body language.
- Consider what body language reflects how we want to show up.
- Adjust our body to match the way we want to show up.

You may have come across the work of Amy Cuddy, well-known for her TED talk entitled *'Your body language may shape who you are'*, the second most watched TED talk ever with sixty-six million views at the time of writing.[38] Her research focuses in depth on how we can use our body to influence how we feel and think, and thus as a powerful tool for being at our best and for personal change.

She states:

> 'Our body language is also speaking to us, to our own inner selves.'[39]

Cuddy's work demonstrates that we can change our habitual patterns by deliberately using our bodies differently. This initiates a feedback loop that leads the brain to adjust its interpretations, its predictions, and consequently our reality. The neuroscience of 'fake it till you make it'.

For a final example of how we can apply right-brain wisdom on a personal level, I'd like to share part of a conversation with a coachee in London's Kensington Gardens.

Lev is leaving his role at a prestigious firm after five years and he isn't sure what he wants to do next. Several things are important to him and they seem to pull him in different directions. Part of him wants to look for another role with high achievement, high reward and high prestige, another part of him wants to do something meaningful for society, and yet another part wants a healthier lifestyle and more happiness as the last five years have taken a toll on his wellbeing. These different forces make it difficult to decide what to do next. As we start our conversation, I leave him a lot of time to talk to give his left brain space to share details while listening and acknowledging.

Walking and talking in Kensington gardens, we suddenly find ourselves on a seven-way crossing in the park. 'Lets pause here for a moment,' I say as we stand at the junction.

'Imagine the path we just walked is your last five years, and the paths in front of you are different possibilities. What do you see when you look at them?'

Lev looks around him for a moment, 'These couple of paths on the right are straight, I can see quite far along them. The other paths are less straight, I am not sure where they lead.'

'I see what you mean, along those ones we can see really far ahead. What else do you see?'

'Some of the paths have more people, some have cyclists, some have dogs or buggies.'

'Even some geese', I add, smiling and pointing to a path on our left. 'This may seem like a strange question, if you let your body choose, what path does it want to take?'

'This one,' he says, and we start to walk along that path.

Lev takes us down the most windy path with little visibility on where it is going. There is no-one else on this path, only some birds. We wander through the trees and suddenly he stops, 'Look! One of the other paths joins up with this one which wasn't visible from the crossing. I guess we cannot always see how the paths will unfold – different journeys can lead to the same destination.'

'What was happening when you chose this path?', I ask.

Lev replies, 'I did not want to go down one of the straight paths, those felt exactly like a repeat of the last five years, no surprises, not good for me, quite standard and boring. My feet absolutely didn't want to go there.'.

'What would you like to do next?', I ask.

'I'd like to continue walking on this path, see what else I find out,' he replies.

We walk along silently and after a while I ask him what he is reflecting on. Lev tells me that his desire to be on the straight path is connected to his upbringing, what he had always seen and heard that success was about. He wants to lead a different life, even though doing so is unsettling, and he isn't sure yet where it will lead. Yet he had felt in his body that this was the right path.

At the end of our discussion, Lev says he wants to come back at the weekend to do the whole walk again.

In this conversation, Lev's body showed him the difference between what he thought he should do, and what he himself, at his core, most wanted to do. Most of us encounter such moments in our life, where we feel pulled in different directions, and they are not easy to navigate. These conflicting forces in us are real.

Fast-forward several years, and I contact Lev to ask his permission to share part of our conversation in this book. He tells me that he did, indeed, go back, this time jogging the entire route we walked. The realization that different journeys can lead to a similar destination, illustrated by the re-joining paths, is still very clear in his mind but, at the time, he did wonder whether this was just luck. He questioned whether we would have had a different conversation with other insights had we walked along different paths. Perhaps you are wondering the same. Of course, this is impossible to know as we cannot rewrite history. My view is that the right brain brings into our awareness what illustrates the message it is trying to convey in that moment. If there had not been re-joining paths, we might have noticed birds re-joining in flight, or dogs running along the grass and re-joining. Lev had come to the same conclusion when he jogged the route.

Some suggestions for conversations such as this. Often, I have found it helps to be outside when accessing right brain wisdom. The combination of space, lots of input for all our senses, and being able to move freely makes it easier for the right brain to lead the conversation. The process defies logic and so our left hemisphere really needs to be relaxed. It doesn't work to march outside in the middle of a meeting with a client, look at a few streets and say, 'so which one do you choose?'. Most people would walk back inside, consider you nuts and hire someone else. In conversations, my approach for relaxing the left brain is to pay attention to it first, to listen and learn from the logic and the internal analysis. You can do this very naturally while walking. After listening attentively, there comes a point where there is no more new information. Then I will remark that there is a lot going on with no clear path forward and suggest that perhaps we could do an experiment together, to try something different and see what we find out.

The next crucial element is to focus on the 'we'. Walking together is a natural way to create a sense of 'we' but note that you cannot just ask questions. If you do, then it is a one-sided conversation as they most probably won't be asking questions of you. You need to offer your own impressions and share what you are experiencing.

Finally, draw on the left brain to support the analysis and interpretation of the information. As we saw earlier, the left brain can be impatient to reach a conclusion. My approach here is to use questions that keep analysis at a high level: 'What thoughts are you having?' or, 'What are you reflecting on?' or, simply, 'What's popping up in your mind?'. Don't seek a full analysis or conclusion so refrain from asking, 'So, which job are you going to apply for?' but, rather, finish with, 'So what are you thinking you might do next?' to conclude the conversation.

My first employer was located outside Amsterdam, in a big house with a small park and a pond that we could walk around. The senior people in the office would walk around the pond in conversation, either together or with their clients. As a young 'rookie' it all looked a bit frivolous to me, yet they clearly understood the value of walking together. I will use this moment to say thanks to my dear friend Mirko, one of those pond walkers, for thirty years of guidance, encouragement and friendship.

Flow of a coaching session using body information

There are many opportunities for tapping into body information. The flow below describes what is generally applicable. You need space to do this work; either a larger office with room to move around, or an outside space.

- Start by identifying the topic of the conversation.

- Give your coachee some time to talk through their thoughts, listen actively, summarize regularly and ask questions for more information. This is a very different start to the coaching session described in the previous chapter. You are listening to the left brain's recounting of events, while using the time to establish a strong connection with your coachee. Active listening is essential, acknowledging what you hear.

- Almost always, there will be a natural place to pause in the conversation and/or in the environment such as a bench to sit on or a unique location (like the junction of seven paths with Lev).

- Now you can briefly summarize what you heard so far and suggest you do an experiment together. Sometimes I say I am following my own gutfeel, and I acknowledge I don't know what this will bring either – are they up for that?

- Based on the topic of your conversation, you will have to formulate an appropriate experiment and question. I can't tell you what to do as a general rule, you have to trust your own right brain to know. What I can say is that it has to be a simple experiment that involves some body movement. The examples in this chapter describe a few different options.

- For this next part, as the coach, you have to be fully and completely present. Hold the space for your coachee. Radiate unconditional positive regard and deep trust in the experience. Hold yourself back from doing any analyzing.

- Don't try to do too much. A complicated experiment doesn't work.

- Offer observations that come from your own body, to model what you are encouraging your coachee to look for.

- In the last ten minutes of the conversation, bring the left brain back in to make sense of it all – keep the conversation high level i.e. 'What thoughts are you having?' Remember, no conclusions.

- Wrap up the conversation by asking what the coachee would like to do next.

Tapping into the wisdom of the right brain with teams

Ravi has recently taken a senior leadership role in a new organization and approaches me to facilitate a team strategy day. His team consists mostly of highly experienced managers, some of whom have been in their role for years and are running their departments independently. He believes in the value of a new level of collaboration in the senior team and wants to use the team strategy day to set the tone.

Part of the agenda for the day is to align on a team vision and then translate that vision into shared goals. Ravi and his team are responsible for major infrastructure projects, some with a horizon of thirty years.

In such a context, it can be especially challenging to stay aligned between departments. A week or a month here and there doesn't immediately matter yet, over time, divergence of priorities, consequent actions and lack of communication can lead to major issues.

Before lunch, the team articulates a shared vision. Everyone seems pleased with the outcome. But during the discussion, a few comments ('If it means this, I don't agree.') indicate to me that there are still some hot issues to iron out.

To explore goals and objectives, we stick a long strip of masking tape to the floor, representing a timeline from today to five years ahead. We start off at the end of the tape, representing where we will be in five years' time. This far in the future, the goals and measurements of success are easy to articulate and include the completion of a big project, the number jobs created, etc. The team is standing together, discussing animatedly, with relaxed postures.

Next, we move back in time, along the masking tape, towards the two-year mark to discuss shared goals for this time. During this movement, some of the group members start to fan out. Some team members stay silent, whilst a smaller group debates actively. My focus is on their body language rather than the content of the conversation, and on using that information to aid the discussion:

'Rob, I am noticing you have moved further out, what is your perspective from there?'

'Mary, you are looking out of the window a lot, what do you see?'

These physical movements, usually unconscious, are signals. Mary voices her doubts about how aligned the rest of the organization is with the goals of the leadership team and this leads to a useful debate.

Rob's first response is, 'I just like standing here'. It can happen that the person was not aware of their movements and feels put on the spot when asked about it.

One of the other team members gently probes, 'Rob, I am really curious to hear your views'.

Rob's second response is that he feels his department is on a different timeline, that he thinks a lot of the two-year goals need to be achieved sooner. He feels disconnected from the team. These are the conversations the team needs to have.

Once the team notices how I am picking up on their body movements, they start using this information themselves. 'Rob, what do you need to take a step towards us or how can we take a step towards you?' When we tune our attention to body information, even without training, most of us can easily start picking up relevant information.

A few suggestions for facilitating a team process in this way. As with walking in the park, it is essential to steer the involvement of both hemispheres to be in a good place for such an exercise. Plan the agenda in a way that first gives the left brain attention, then acknowledge and listen to its input. Invite the right brain into the conversation by, for example, using some visuals. With Ravi's team, as part of the earlier conversation about vision, we had done an exercise with post-its, a simple way to make ideas visual. We had also managed the process such that everyone was engaged and heard, stimulating an experience of 'we' throughout the morning.

When tuning into body information, the most important thing to have in mind is to keep it very simple and to trust the right brain to show you and/or others what is relevant. Make it a practice not to dismiss anything that is observed, even if the relevance is not immediately clear.

As an alternative to working with a timeline, another approach is to nominate an object in the room, e.g. a chair, as the team's objective and ask people to stand somewhere in the room to represent where they each stand vis-à-vis the objective. A wealth of information is revealed in observing how far people stand from the chair, how quickly they move to their position, who stands near each other and who doesn't.

Embodying dynamics in a simple way reveals forces that impact the day-to-day functioning of a team yet are hard to put into words. Making such forces visible and factual facilitates useful team conversations that strengthen a team's ability to work well together and deliver results.

Tapping into the wisdom of the right brain in our relationships with others

Even when we don't pay attention, our brains are taking in body information. In Chapter One, we touched on the discovery of mirror neurons and the process through which our bodies mirror the physical experiences of others. If we take in information from others all the time, even if a lot of it is outside of our awareness, perhaps there are ways to access such information.

This is an example of a conversation aimed at doing just that, by literally stepping into someone else's shoes (or rather, sitting in their chair).

Maria, one of my coachees, is keen to improve a difficult working relationship with her colleague, Simon. She tells me about her experience of working with Simon and what she finds challenging.

I suggest we could explore Simon's perspective for a bit. 'Are you up for that?', I ask her, and she agrees.

I invite her to get up and sit in another chair, 'Can you show me how Simon would typically sit?' She looks a little puzzled. I demonstrated a few different positions while saying 'Does he lean forward or backwards, does he smile a lot?'

Maria proceeds to fold her arms behind her head and starts looking rather bored. 'He sits like this,' she says.

'I am going to talk to you as if you are Simon, just keep sitting like him and say whatever pops up in your mind.'

'Hi Simon,' I say, 'nice to meet you.'

'Nice to meet you too,' Simon (Maria) replies.

'Can you tell me something about what is important to you?'

Simon (Maria): 'I would really like to build something lasting in the coming years. This is likely my last big role before I retire, and I want to accomplish something good.'

'That sounds important, I can relate to that,' I respond, 'and I understand you are working with Maria'. He (she) nods. 'What is that like for you?'

'Well, I get the feeling that she wants to score some big points fast and isn't concerned much with the long-term implications. Her motivations are quite different to mine.'

'If you could ask her for something, what would you like to ask?'

'I would really like her not to jump to conclusions so quickly and to listen more.'

At this point, I invite Maria to stand up and sit back in her own chair and ask for her reaction to what Simon said. We go back and forth a few times, and each time, by sitting in another chair and emulating Simon's body posture, Maria steps into Simon's world. Maria realizes that her actions have not inspired trust and she figures out how she could adjust her own behavior to address this issue. She recognizes that Simon has a point, that her outlook is different than his, yet she is confident there is a lot of common ground between their motives and their values. Having an open and honest conversation with Simon to establish common ground would be her first step to take. She knows she is not a good listener, and this had come up in previous stakeholder relationships. She is keen to make 'understand first, then be understood' her new attitude.

This conversation helped Maria to see the situation from Simon's point of view and used body information to make this possible. Sometimes, if we ask ourselves what the perspective of the other person might be, that is enough to give us a fresh look on the situation. But if positions are entrenched, and are affecting you personally, this can quite hard. By then, your brain is making sure your senses pick up only the signals that confirm your opinion. So we need to be a bit more crafty to trick ourselves to look at the situation from someone else's perspective.

Examples of simple questions that still involve a subtle change of position are:

- If you were a fly on the wall of this conversation / meeting, what would you see?

- If you were walking past this meeting room, what would you hear?
- Your organization's headquarters and CEO are based in 'Oslo', what would Oslo's view on this matter be?

To further prompt body information, such questions can be complemented with an action. You can physically leave the meeting room and walk past it. Or get out of your chairs and stand by the wall, imitating a fly's position. Travelling to Oslo, or wherever your organizations' headquarters are, seems a little unreasonable but Oslo can be brought into the room by talking about what it is like to be there; describing the view from the headquarters, or what you see inside the building.

In Maria's conversation, we go one step further to use body information from someone else to generate insights. We often notice things about other people yet don't actively process them. It is rather surprising what imitating someone's body posture can generate. It really can help us to start understanding someone else's perspective.

Such a process is challenging to do on your own and much easier with the help of someone else. That other person also generates your 'we experience', supports the involvement of the right brain, and can help you notice new information.

We do have to be mindful not to jump to conclusions about what is going on for another person based on what we experience when we take on their body posture – our interpretation is, of course, still entirely of our own making, based on our own stories and experiences. But as long we realize we are still making assumptions, and offer our experiences as input rather than the truth, I don't see an issue with that. Why not use all the data we have, including body information?

So, to sum up...

The right brain is a source of knowledge and wisdom, with access to information that the left side of our brain does not have. This information, accessed via the body, is referred to in this book as tapping into the wisdom of the right brain. One of the main things that body information brings us is awareness of our emotions and the emotions of others, making the right brain essential for our social awareness and capacity for empathy.

Some people are more attuned to their body information than others, and are therefore generally more aware of their own and others' emotions. Some are naturally gifted in this area and develop the ability to read input from their body from an early age, almost instinctively. We can all learn to become more aware of our body information, step by step, and explore the learnings from body information in simple ways.

Think of a colleague who has been irritating you lately. When you observe them in a meeting room, take a moment to sit exactly like them. You might notice you feel very tired in that position. Then you suddenly remember they have been first in the office each morning for the past two weeks, and you start wondering what is going on. Once that realization is there, you will be curious to find out more. The left brain has an important role to play in analyzing, making sense of body information, and identifying next steps.

Working with body information typically follows these steps:

- Pause and pay attention to a body sensation.
- If the left brain kicks in to dismiss your awareness, simply say to yourself 'this will only take a moment'.

- Follow the body sensation, when you have the urge to yawn, rub your eyes, look back or stand up, do so.
- Invite your left brain in by asking yourself, 'What could this be about?', stimulating your curiosity.

In addition to emotional awareness, we can learn much more from our body. Our brain is constantly predicting what our body needs based on an enormous amount of information in any given moment including our physical state, the demands of our environment, our thoughts and perception, our beliefs, our hopes and dreams. With specific techniques, we can use the body to express all of that complexity and thus gain valuable insights about what is important to us. Often these insights include information that was previously not in our conscious awareness.

We can also use reverse this process and use our body to transmit information to our brain. Our brain primes our body to behave in the way it believes is necessary. Sometimes, this input is outdated or not fit for purpose to who we want to be right now. So we have the ability to 'override' the priming and use our body in a different way. By doing so, we send our brain a new message about who we are which ultimately impacts future priming.

The next chapter looks at how these powerful right brain techniques can support leaders in practical ways, with the difficult leadership challenges of today's world. One of those areas where information of the body can be a game changer, is in making diversity and inclusion a successful reality.

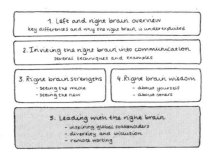

Leading with the right brain

This final chapter explores how leaders can embrace the strengths and wisdom of the right brain to specifically address the challenges that characterize the 21st century.

First, we will review how the right brain supports leaders to inspire global stakeholders, in-person and on virtual platforms. Next, we will see how, by working with the qualities of the right brain, we can make a step change towards harnessing the value of diversity. Finally, we will look at the part that the right brain plays in building more sustainable organizations, as activating the right brain can make remote working more fulfilling, more enjoyable and better for our well-being.

Many leaders shoulder large responsibilities, obligations, and expectations. Today's challenges are not simple. Being a leader is often rewarding and a great privilege, and yet it also can be tough, lonely and frustrating. It is my hope that in reading and learning about your right brain, you will be inspired to access a power that you might not have previously been aware of. And doing so might even help to lighten the load. Aside from valuable new insights and perspectives, working with the right brain brings a sense playfulness, enjoyment and ease that, in itself, is precious in a busy life.

Inspiring global stakeholders

In May 2021, the dean of MIT Sloan School of Management, David Smittlein, organized a forum with alumni to share and discuss the school's view on the future of management education. After more than a full year of virtual education and virtual working, this resulted in a lively debate. I was curious about school's view on any change in leadership qualities required for the next decade with the increase of virtual working, even beyond the pandemic. It is not that in-person leadership has become obsolete, not at all, but the role of the virtual platform to engage with stakeholders around the world is growing – whether in 1:1 meetings, team meetings or larger company-wide forums. So how does this trend impact critical leadership qualities?

Dean Schmittlein positioned that, in his view, there is an increasing need for leaders to excel in visioning.[40] I was intrigued, for what else is visioning other than painting a picture of the future – creating a visual for what is to come – and thus a way to engage the right brain of employees, clients, investors or other stakeholders?

We often say that we follow leaders who engage both our hearts and our minds. Traditionally, for important moments, leaders have always shown up in person to inspire, such as presidential candidates who tour the country. Why? As referenced in Chapter One, being in the same room with a leader, hearing their words and simultaneously 'getting a feel' for them whilst using all our senses, that is what fully convinces us about a person and inspires us to follow them.

During the pandemic, we quickly made enormous progress in engaging minds using the virtual platforms. We learned how to have efficient discussions with new virtual meeting protocols (raising your hand, using the chat); using tools such as Trello boards to increase team effectiveness; and presenting materials effortlessly over Zoom or Microsoft Teams. And yet, engaging hearts virtually was, and is, a much greater hurdle. This is not a surprise – we are not neurobiologically programmed to do so as we can't send or receive the same signals with all our senses when communicating through a screen. As leaders, inspiring others to follow in a virtual world is an altogether different ballgame.

When we refer to 'engaging hearts and minds', despite how it sounds, this doesn't equate to literally engaging two different organs, the brain and the heart, but rather to fully engaging both the left and right side of the brain.

As illustrated in the previous chapter, the right brain is the door to our emotional experience through its connection to our body. Being in the same room together is a powerful way to engage the senses and, more broadly, the whole body. This stimulates an information flow into the right brain and drives our emotional experience. But if we can't be in the same room together, we need to engage the right brain differently. That starts by inviting the right brain into the conversations, by speaking its language through – you guessed it – visuals.

I need to tackle a popular misconception about visioning. When I ask someone to describe a situation with a metaphor or an image, some reply that they 'don't do images'. As everyone has right hemisphere, which processes in visual imagery, this is utter nonsense. It seems to me we have come to associate the ability to create images with art and have attributed the skills of 'painting a picture', literally or figuratively, to artists. I suppose the good news, therefore, is that we are all artists in our right brains. Kidding aside, there certainly is a difference between people in how naturally they talk in metaphors and images seem to translate more easily into words for those who readily talk in metaphor. Yet, when prompted, everyone can access images and develop the skills to communicate visually, as shown in the many examples of Chapter 2.

Given the importance of engaging the left and the right side of the brain when influencing or inspiring others, we could even turn this around and argue that if no image emerges to describe something, it implies a lack of clarity. To put it boldly, if we cannot illustrate our personal, team, business or industry vision with an image, we don't actually have a vision.

Let's look at a few examples to illustrate. Firstly, I'll put myself to the test. What image illustrates my vision for 'Leading with the right brain?' You have already seen it, it's on the cover of the book. My vision for this book is to unleash your personal genie – this giant hidden power withinyour right brain. The genie comes to life as an image, usually a big blue dude, just as the power of your right brain materializes with image. And, just as you need your body to release the genie by rubbing your hand against the lamp, the right brain's wisdom can be accessed by using your body.

For full transparency, this image didn't just appear to me on the spot, it took some work to find it and I later realized that an interview with Jill Bolte Taylor that I read years ago, had inspired my use of the image.[41] You might have to go through some iterations to find the right image to describe your vision, project or goal which ultimately is part of the process of finding clarity.

Here is a second example: a senior financial advisor shared how he used an image to get his point across. With the aim of convincing a client that he was best positioned to support them, he had shared his proposed step by step approach. He was then asked the following  question, 'Now that you have shared your approach, why would we still need to hire you?'. His reply, 'Let's compare sharing my approach to me sharing the recipe to my grandmother's Bouillabaisse. Even though you know the recipe, there is no way you can make her tasty Bouillabaisse without me.'.

Recently, one of my coachees was practising her pitch for the next round of funding. In a fast-growing start-up, securing funding takes a lot of time for the CEO. For advanced software companies, their product can be quite intangible, and she found it challenging to communicate to new investors what their company was really about. As a result, in the pitch presentations, a lot of time was lost on investors challenging her company and her approach. Adding few good images showing her vision for how their product would change the industry, brought about a shift in the discussions from challenging (pushing her into the defensive) to curious and constructive.

Next time you are preparing to communicate a strategy, to position a new initiative or to give someone a responsibility, ask yourself what image would illustrate what you are hoping to accomplish. Equally, when your boss asks you to work on a project, ask them to give you an image. If they don't have one ready, you can come up with your own and can test your understanding by sharing your image to make sure you are aligned. For example, when you are tasked with improving a process, verify if you are to give it a new overcoat, an entirely new outfit or just iron out the wrinkles. Your boss might say that they are not fully sure yet; it will surely be more than ironing out the wrinkles but how extensive the new wardrobe needs to be is one of the key questions. This gives you a starting point for outlining options before diving in too deeply.

Sometimes a good visual comes to us immediately, sometimes we need a bit of time and/or some iterations. Your gutfeel will tell you when the image is right, and it is easy to test with others to see if it resonates. All the techniques from Chapter Two are useful to inspire visuals. I would recommend everyone to keep a good set of pictures in their desk drawer (see Appendix). And, furthermore, to find out which of your colleagues easily think in metaphors – they will always be a willing thought partner to find a good visual.

To sum up this part on inspiring global stakeholders: leaders have many responsibilities, including inspiring others to follow them, and this requires engaging the whole person – mind and heart, left and right brain. Traditionally, leaders have relied heavily on being in person to inspire others, using their physical presence and personal charisma to engage their audience's right brains. If leaders can't meet their stakeholders in person, the best way to engage their right brains is through visioning: painting a picture of what they want to achieve. Arguably, it is always smart, whether in-person or virtual, to use images as well as words when communicating. In a virtual setting, it is the lack of other means to engage the right brain that makes visioning such an essential leadership skill.

Harnessing the value of diversity and inclusion

A few years ago I was told the following story by one of my coachees. A top-performer, my coachee was highly intelligent and relatively young in his position. For his development, he had been told he needed to make 'more impact in the room' during meetings. With this story, he was trying to illustrate why this was so hard for him.

'Yda,' he said to me, 'you know the kind of gathering where departments get together for some food and a senior management talk. Typically, these happen in a large meeting room and everyone stands around chatting in small groups. When I walk into the room, those small groups quietly close in front of me. You have no idea how difficult it is to keep walking and stay in that room, when all I see are people's backs.'.

My coachee is an African man, working for a large multinational organization.

Every time I remember his story, even as I write it down now, it is a jolt to the system. My muscles tense up, my arms close in and I feel frozen. He makes me see something that is normally invisible to me. I am afraid to move for fear this momentary awareness, tough as it is, will disappear when I do.

Listening to his story was a humbling experience. As a woman, studying and working in predominantly male environments my whole life, I thought I had some understanding of the diversity challenge yet, in that moment, I realized that I had not come close to understanding the extent of exclusion that others experience. In an excellent TED talk, Michael Kimmer says:

'Privilege is invisible for those who have it.'[42]

As a white, educated, straight, cisgender, slim, and healthy woman, I am pretty much drowning in privilege. Having a glimpse of my coachee's experience, and seeing a familiar environment from his perspective, was as enlightening as it was shocking and a forceful reminder of how much we don't, can't, or won't see.

For many leaders and their organizations, Diversity and Inclusion (D&I) is top of the agenda. For clarity, with 'Diversity' I mean the mix of employees along all dimensions of diversity (gender, race, sexuality, religion, etc.). 'Inclusion' refers to the ability to make the mix work and build high performing teams and organizations with a diverse workforce. While it is certainly challenging to recruit a diverse mix of employees, my clients report that 'inclusion' is an even more elusive challenge. Even when employees of diverse backgrounds and identities join an organization with all the qualifications needed for a role, they frequently struggle to become successful. The organization of my coachee above is a case in point. They have worked hard to recruit a diverse workforce yet that in itself doesn't create an inclusive culture.

How can we be inclusive when our bodies are so excruciatingly exclusive?

The general consensus is that one of the key challenges for inclusion is unconscious bias, the deep-rooted beliefs and attitudes we hold due to living in an unequal society. Our unconscious (implicit) biases lead us to make instinctive assumptions and judgements about others and we behave accordingly without consciously realizing we do. Explicit bias, deliberately excluding or discriminating against others, also exists yet is a different kind of issue. Implicit bias, for example, is assuming a doctor is a man or assuming a nurse is a woman. Our brains predict our environment based on those assumptions. If you have been in a hospital waiting for a nurse, you would have very likely experienced a measure of surprise if a man appeared in the doorway, let alone a large one with many tattoos. Many of us want to be inclusive and even believe we are inclusive, yet due to unconscious bias we continue to behave in exclusive ways. For a fascinating (and possibly sobering) look into your own bias, I recommend doing the *Harvard Implicit Association Test*.[43]

So far, relying on our intellect to change deeply ingrained behaviors has proven to be an unsuccessful route. Many organizations have embarked on unconscious bias training (UBT) in the last decade, hoping to make employees aware of bias and thereby reducing the resulting behaviors that typically make someone feel excluded, offended, belittled or worse. You might have done some UBT yourself and, if so, you will likely have experienced that nothing much changes afterwards. Though well intended, and despite the enormous amounts of investment in it, the overwhelming evidence is that increasing awareness of bias doesn't generate much change.[44]

Shocking though it was to hear about my coachee's experience in his office meetings, when recalling the intricate, ultra-fast, connections between the brain and the body as discussed in the last chapter, it is not surprising that our bodies show our biases before anything else, and without us realizing what is happening.

Yet could there be a way to use this in reverse? You will recall my mention, in Chapter Four, of Dr Amy Cuddy's work.[45] She focused on increasing presence with powerful body poses, evoking a different response in ourselves and our environment through the way we hold our bodies. Could we use the same principle for inclusiveness? In other words, can we build our way to inclusion by using our bodies?

Yes, I believe so. Having shared my hypotheses on the matter with several senior executives, one of them, Ray, reported the following. When interviewing a new potential senior hire, he had only realized she was of African descent when she, Sara, walked in the door. As I had recently told him the story of the African coachee, it was still fresh in his mind and Ray told me that as he sat behind his desk, he noticed he started leaning back, intending to take a relaxed posture. 'In that moment,' Ray said, 'I stopped myself and leaned forward instead. I wanted to indicate openness and invitation rather than power and authority. It felt a bit odd for an instant, but I did it anyway. We had a fantastic first discussion, and after several more conversations, she eventually joined the team'.

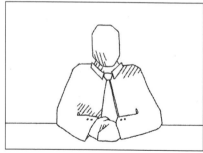

I have come to the following view. We, as humans, have a wonderful ability to collaborate, work and live in groups. Historically, until very recently, these groups have been homogeneous, made up of our own tribe, race and culture and, consequently, our biological make-up is such that we are naturally inclusive to those like us, and naturally exclusive to those unlike us. This is a deeply embedded pattern in our biology and our bodies behave accordingly, though we are completely unaware that we are doing so. I am not passing any judgement here, we have simply evolved in this way because it was necessary. However, I do firmly believe we will not be able to rationalize our way into an inclusive society, at least not at the pace we want or need to, as being exclusive is so deeply embedded in our habits. We have to show ourselves the way forward and we can use our bodies to do so. This requires leadership on a personal, team, organizational and state level.

Instead of being a victim of our unconscious prejudices, experiencing the world through our biases and living by behaviors that re-enforce the same patterns, we can use our bodies to change the entire experience. There are many examples of this phenomena: when we put a pencil in our mouth horizontally and our lips automatically form the shape of a smile, our body and brain recognize the movement and we immediately feel more positive and respond differently. Equally, when we lean towards a person, we listen more attentively and straight away take more interest in what they have to say.

So what kind of body language is 'inclusive'? In *The Silent language of Leaders*,[46] Carol Kinsey Goman, introduces a framework for body language. She writes that when first introduced to a leader, we immediately and unconsciously assess him or her for warmth and authority. For the body language of inclusion she highlights a subset of the warmer side of body language: eye contact, smiling, head nods and body orientation.

What is essential to appreciate is that we form an opinion about a person based on their body language, even before they have spoken a word. Research from Princeton University[47] suggests this happens as fast as in 0.1 seconds. Many people talk about seven seconds in this context though I couldn't trace the original reference. What is undisputed though is that our bodies communicate much faster than our words. First impressions are highly relevant for inclusivity, they can create a virtuous cycle of collaboration or an instant cycle of rejection that is hard to stop. Ray's real-time realization and action to change his body language may well have been that crucial instant where the collaboration with Sara was set on the right path.

This is the game changer on inclusivity. Consciously adjusting our body information so our bodies signal inclusivity in first impressions and beyond, even if the rest of us – especially our brain – hasn't fully caught up yet.

Please pause a moment and really take this in. It sounds so simple. It isn't.

Taking such an action requires the active participation of your right brain and the collaboration of your left brain. Remember that whole body information enters your right brain first; your right brain is focused on the present moment – not on the past or the future – and your left brain is quick to dismiss right brain input. Ray noticed he was starting to lean back in his chair as it was happening. If he had been thinking about something else, for example, the required follow-up from the client call he'd just finished, whether he should introduce Sara to some colleagues after the conversation, about a major issue on one of his projects, or anything else, he would have missed the moment. All of the above are relevant topics to occupy his thoughts and, at first sight, a small shift in body language seems inconsequential in comparison.

In other words, a small bit of information that originates from your right brain needs to be acknowledged and prioritized in the present moment, in the midst of a whirlwind of thoughts, so that you can take the action you want to take with your body language. This requires a high level of awareness of and control over your thoughts at any given moment. Not many people have this level of control. Having known Ray for some time now, I can safely say that he does not have that level of control. Neither do I for that matter.

But Ray is smart, and if something is presented to him with a solid logic, he will pay attention to it in relevant moments. A first interview with a senior female candidate, who then also turned out to be a racial minority, qualified as a highly relevant moment. His left brain was already engaged with the idea that this body language adjustment could be relevant in the context of diversity and inclusion, and he was curious enough to experiment. That combination made him notice his body movement in the moment and take action. So, if your rational left brain is already convinced enough to be curious, you might treat that small bit of body information differently and realize that you can act on it. Ray told me, after his interview with Sara, that he was convinced his body language at the start made a difference. I asked him how he knew that. 'I am not sure,' he said, 'but I knew I had established a connection. It was my objective to get her interested in the role, in joining my team – and she was.'.

'So now that you have had this one positive experience, where you noticed your body information and adjusted it effectively, how are you going to use this in future situations?'

Ray replied 'Actually, I am now using it with everyone, always leaning forwards instead of leaning backwards. I realized I was leaning backwards far too often. It would be impossible to decide for each conversation what to do so now I always lean forward'.

He is of course completely right. It would be much too complex to determine during interactions when to adjust our body and when not. Instead, always making our body information inviting to overcome our exclusive body instincts, is a much more effective approach.

Just to be clear, I am not talking about ignoring our body instincts in all situations. For example, please continue crossing the street to avoid someone you find threatening. Whether they are a threat or not, better safe than sorry. But at work, in the meeting room or by the coffee machine, we can make it a practice to act differently.

By consciously adjusting our body to be inclusive in all settings, and experiencing the results, we are then rapidly impacting our brain's predictions of what is needed in a situation. And those predictions, in turn, impact the preparation of our body – to the point where we will automatically turn toward instead of turn away.

It is a well-known fact that a leader's behavior (conscious or otherwise) has enormous impact on others, and naturally this includes their body language. When you, as the leader, always frown during meetings, others will do the same to project authority. When you consistently open your circle during Friday lunch gatherings to invite a newcomer to join, especially someone from a diverse background, this will become the norm in your organization. Your behavior sets the example for others and, as crucial, it impacts your own experience. When you tilt your head and nod when a woman speaks up in a meeting, you affect your own level of interest in what she says, you will listen better and are more likely to hear something relevant.

In short, we have the possibility to make diversity and inclusion a successful reality by adapting our body language. This requires overriding our automatic exclusive behaviors. Through our bodies, we can change our behavior, our mindset, our beliefs and ultimately our reality and that of those around us *today*. If you are not in a leadership role yet, please don't wait for your boss to set the example. You too can act now. It may sometimes feel a little awkward at first. Good! That means you are pushing through that unconscious bias that might lead you to unconsciously turn away. You may not always be fast enough to turn towards someone every time, smile, nod or make positive eye-contact. Don't worry. Every time you notice you were not fast enough is a step in the right direction.

Sustainability and the right brain

Alongside diversity and inclusion, it's hard to imagine an executive who does not have sustainability on their mind. Next to the strategic questions that sustainability raises for their business, my clients are also wondering about practical structural matters such as how much time employees should spend in the office, how to plan for prime office real estate, how much to fly, just to name a few.

Part of their decision-making process on such practical matters is impacted by the belief that working from home results in less connection to colleagues, and consequently negatively affects employee engagement. The strong connection between employee engagement and business performance has been firmly established by the Gallup organization.[48] So while working from home might be good for the environment, it likely affects business performance negatively. In the first pandemic lockdowns, with everyone working from home and spending long hours on video conferences, many people experienced loneliness despite working the whole day with others via their screens. In 2021, so many employees voluntarily left their work, this trend was called 'The Great Attrition'.[49] In that same year, employee engagement in the US fell for the first time in a decade.[50] Executives are right to worry about employee engagement in the context of working from home.

For one of our client organizations, we run a yearly program supporting high-potential leaders. The success of this program is highly dependent on the strength of the community we are able to build amongst the group while they work together for a period of about nine months. Pre-pandemic, the community-building formula consisted of bringing the group together at the start of the program in a lovely French chateau and, after a day of stimulating content and conversations, serving a tasty dinner accompanied by a good bottle of wine. Not particularly original yet a very effective formula to build a community.

When the first lockdown hit, we were in the middle of one of these programs and scrambled to deliver a day-and a-half-long workshop over Zoom. Participants were regularly stepping in and out to deal with work or home emergencies, sometimes attending with little kids on their laps, it was very far from ideal. By May 2020, even though the first lockdowns were slowly ending, it was clear that regular business travel would take a long time to recover. We were faced with the simple question: can we build a real community when we can only work virtually? If not, the program could not continue. Most people at the time, when asked this question, would say no, that is not possible. In fact, also today, most people feel this doesn't work.

But I know that it is possible. We can build strong virtual communities; groups of people that do intense work together, contribute to each other's wellbeing and happiness, and yet never meet in person.

While I don't believe in, or advocate for, 100% virtual working; I am convinced that we can make virtual work rewarding and enriching, not simply efficient. If so, this would have far-reaching implications for how businesses can be organized and could be a substantial contributor to a more sustainable world.

The essential ingredient for building a virtual community is full and active engagement in the work together. As discussed earlier in the context of visioning, full engagement requires participation of our left and right hemispheres. But here we are looking for something even more, we are looking for full *and active* engagement. It is like the difference between being captivated by watching a show and actually being on the stage, immersing yourself fully in creating the experience. There is a feeling of satisfaction and fulfilment that comes from participating and collaborating with other human beings, whether in sports, arts, business or any other arena of life. Our bodies play a crucial role in such collaborations. Please take a moment and remember a time where you were totally engrossed in collaboration, being in the same place and working together, or doing a team sport, fully present with each other and the activity. It is likely that such a memory will also trigger a physical sensation, as if your body remembers the moment too.

Achieving 100% full and active engagement is much harder virtually. There are still more distractions at home such as doorbells ringing for deliveries. Or, when in a virtual meeting while at work, colleagues popping into your office. As we are not fully visible to each other on video meetings, it is tempting to do things that in regular meetings would be ludicrous or at least very odd. Imagine walking on a treadmill, stapling papers together, rearranging your desk, or quickly adding some anchovies to your on-line shopping basket before the deadline during an in-person meeting. We can be wearing shorts and flip flops below the professionally-dressed top half of our body, in yet another way being only half there. We feel we are being efficient when multi-tasking, but this is largely an illusion. Switching between activities consumes brain energy as does resisting distractions. These additional distractions, whether taken or not, make the required level of engagement challenging when working virtually.

Furthermore, we are not biochemically wired to have the same physical response to seeing someone over video as we are when we see them in person. I realized it most acutely when finally visiting my parents again after the pandemic. We had spoken and done video calls during the lockdowns, stayed in contact even more than we usually do. When I saw them again, we were surprised to find that we were quite caught up with each other's lives, there wasn't much to discuss. I had imagined this big emotional reunion, yet within five minutes it felt completely normal to be around each other. But, later in the afternoon, when we were sitting together in the garden, cups of tea in hand, each reading our own book, I could feel my body quietly humming with pleasure.

Future generations might respond differently to virtual working than we currently do. We still struggle to adjust our expectations about human communication to the restrictions of a video call. But when growing up with something from birth onwards, it is a different ballgame. If you have ever watched a five-year-old with a touch screen, you will know what I mean. They don't use a touch screen; they interact with the touch screen. When we are born with a technology, it seems our body and brain develop differently around that technology than if we learn it at a later stage in our lives. If this is true for touch screens, why not for virtual working? It is not a big stretch of the imagination to expect that the engagement and satisfaction of communicating through a screen will be different for future generations.

So how do we create virtual communities now, while our bodies and brains are not yet adjusted? The recipe we use relies on *three key ingredients*. We know this recipe works as we use it several times per year. And because it works, we now have participants on our virtual program from all over the world, enriching the community and the dynamics, and creating a draw to the community in their own right.

The first ingredient is to activate the right side of the brain as quickly as possible and allow participants to get to know each other through right brain connections. This is, in a way, replacing the body connection from being in the same room together with right brain communication. We use a variety of ways to do this, not just one, and every piece of discussion has a visual and active element.

To illustrate how this works: when the group meets for the first time in a virtual workshop, we do the normal introductions very fast, one sentence per person. 'Hi, I am Sam, I work in London and my focus in on healthcare.' This satisfies the left brain's need for information. Subsequently we invite the right brain into the meeting in a variety of ways. For example, we may ask participants how they view their next leadership role and to annotate their position on the Zoom Whiteboard; or we invite them to use the 'feeling good – doing good' framework for a 1:1 breakout discussion (see Chapter 3); or we introduce a series of topics and ask them to show, with annotations, what interests them most by sizing a circle accordingly. All of these are exercises are designed to be both visual, active and interactive.

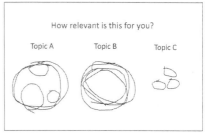

At the end of the first day we ask participants to find and share an object from their home that describes a key part of their personality, to tell the story behind the object and explain what part of their personality it represents. Objects (see Chapter Two) in of themselves continue to stimulate right-brain participation. Bringing an object from your home is especially powerful because it brings the rest of your environment into the video meeting. This year, someone showed the recently-laid eggs from their chicken, someone else a favourite chair in their home, another one a small statue that represented a special memory. Sharing a piece of your home is not possible to do during in-person meetings and adds a unique flavour to the virtual environment. So it becomes a new and exciting space, not just an attempt to replicate an in-person meeting.

The second essential ingredient for a virtual community is to meet regularly and work on current challenges together, so the impact of the community can be immediately felt in someone's day.

There is one extraordinary advantage to virtual working which is that, without the need for travel, it is much easier to bring people together again. Traditionally, it has always been a major hurdle for development experiences to meet more than once. People are busy, life is full of surprises – it is nearly impossible to bring people together in the same constellation multiple times if they are not in the same office or country. And yet development is seldom a one-off. Embedding new behaviors, beliefs, perspectives is not done overnight. Change takes time.

Typically, consensus dictates that development workshops are better held in a different location than at the participants' office space to minimize work distractions (hence we call them off-sites). When everyone travels to an off-site location, the usual approach is then also to maximize group time. 'Let's have a two-day workshop instead of a one-day and take time to do a lot of exercises so participants can practice new behaviors before they get back to the "real world".' I am sure you have had your fair share of off-sites with role plays, real plays, learning groups and the like. While distance reduces distractions, distance also provides a barrier to change. We might have some good learning and practice about being a better listener at an off-site yet still not be able to change behaviors in the office. Our automatic pilot is so powerful that, when back in our normal context, it is much harder to do something new or different.

Virtual working changes this construct completely. We can bring people together more frequently and, in addition, everything we work on collaboratively can become more easily embedded in the workplace. After all, we are sitting on the same chair, looking at the same screen – the environment does not change for our 'offsite'. For such virtual work sessions, we typically organize in smaller sub-groups of three to five participants.

For example, picture a group of four leaders spending one hour together on Zoom on a Monday morning, discussing a particularly challenging work situation that one of them, Adam, is facing. Adam realizes that, due to the large interests at stake in his situation, he has started focusing on and worrying about things that are outside his control. This is taking up a lot of his time and energy and he is not having the impact he wants at this crucial time. With the help of the others, he identifies a few good actions to take. One of the other participants also realizes where she can exert more control in her work situation, and a few actions she would like to take to accomplish that. Everyone logs off the call, continues with their day and the actions that they have helped each other to find can be implemented immediately.

The third essential ingredient of building a virtual community is showing up for each other. The participants in our program are based all over the world – their day-to-day work environments have little or no overlap. Their roles are demanding, and their calendars are full, so they make the time to show up for these meetings because they choose to, for themselves and for each other. This is the true hallmark of a community; you show up because you are as happy to give as you are to receive.

Interactions need to be structured so that there is real exchange and collaboration, inspiring the active engagement mentioned earlier. One of the most impactful ways of achieving this is by orchestrating problem-solving within a metaphor, using both left and right brain qualities. For example, we ask participants what metaphor captures the complexity of their career. One of them, Mia, says she feels like she is on a cruise ship on open sea. There is plenty of entertainment around her; she could go endlessly from swimming pool to dinner party to cabaret performances. But she is restless with no idea of where she is going and no control over the direction of the ship. Take a moment to imagine yourself on that cruise ship - what would you do?

One of the other participants says he would go upstairs to the bridge, where the captain steers the ship, and take control of the wheel. Another one suggests taking one of the lifeboats and jump off the ship. We ask Mia if she wants to stay on the ship or find land? Mia immediately replies she wants to go on land. 'Is any land good?', someone inquires, 'For example, would you be happy to find yourself in Antarctica?' 'No', Mia replies, 'I don't want to get off the ship for the sake of getting off, I want to navigate to the right land'. The group then discusses that she can learn to navigate either from the captain's bridge, or by learning to read the stars. What resonates most with Mia is to learn how to read the stars and in the subsequent months, Mia engages with different constellations of people to get a much clearer map of her universe. By doing so, she develops her ability to see possibilities and feels more in control of her direction. As you are reading this, part of you may think, 'how is it a new idea to engage with stakeholders to understand your career path?'. That is not the point. The point lies in Mia's seeing the meaning of these conversations in way that resonates with her, and her consequent motivation to take action.

Collaborating in metaphors is the closest we have come to virtually creating the experience, the feeling, the satisfaction of working together in-person. Naturally we would not aim to have such an experience in every conversation, in the same way that we don't expect to have a creative, collaborative, generative collaboration in every in-person interaction. However, knowing it is possible in the virtual environment, and understanding the ingredients to make it happen, challenges the belief that working from home negatively affects employee engagement and creates the space for organizations to fundamentally shift their ways of working.

How the right brain can support leaders in the 21st century, a recap

The strengths and wisdom of the right brain can uniquely support leaders to address the many challenges that characterize the 21st century. We have explored three specific applications:

- the use of images to strengthen visioning and influence global stakeholders, especially relevant on the virtual platform;
- the use of the body to become an inclusive leader and make diversity a successful reality;

- the activation of the right brain to make remote working more fulfilling, for example by collaborating within metaphors.

With our left-brain competences and qualities, we effectively navigate most of our day-to-day. Yet when we are stuck in our thinking, in our behaviors, or in our beliefs, we need to activate our right brain.

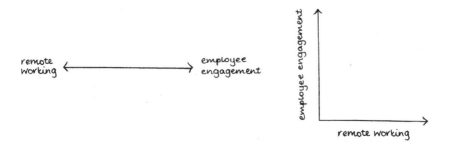

Through the perspective of our right brain, we can see a path where remote working does not compromise employee engagement and business performance. We can be excited about a new responsibility, and equally daunted or even scared by it. We can entertain a possibility that we might be able to work less and bring in more business.

To be the best we can be we need both the left and the right sides of our brain. A viewpoint I hope you share after reading this book. The heart of the matter is that the left side of our brain will inevitably fall into the powerplay of left *or* right. To bring both sides of our brain to the party, *and* benefit from the unique qualities of *both* hemispheres, requires **leading with the right side of the brain.**

Appendix

Following the techniques and examples described in the book, these are the various tools that can be used to invite the right brain into conversations.

Images. There are many sets of images available. This is a selection of those that I have come across over the years. They are each slightly different and have also different price levels.

- The Visual explorer from the Centre of Creative Leadership (CCL) comes in different sets and sizes. See https://shop.ccl.org/usa/tools and scroll down to visual explorer for the full offering. The special edition also comes with a digital version, see https://cclinnovation.org/innovate/explore-ccl-labs-beta-products/visual-explorer-special-edition/. This is a lovely and very broad set of images that can be used in many situations. I have found the playing cards size and digital version especially useful. They tend to be expensive.
- Barefoot coaching has a set of coaching cards that can be found at http://www.barefootcoachingcards.co.uk/picture-cards. This is a postcard size set of good quality and

reasonably-priced cards. It has fewer images that illustrate negative emotions or experiences.

- Metafox produces deep picture coaching cards https:// metafox.eu/deep-pictures/. It is also a postcard size set of good quality, good value cards, with fewer images that illustrate negative emotions or experiences.
- The Dixit board game comes with a set of imaginary playing cards. These are a bit different to a set of pictures yet also work well to invite in the right brain.

Objects. For working with a set of objects, you will have to create your own. Chapter 3 shows what my set of objects looks like, the tangible set and the virtual set. To put it together, I raided the children's toy cupboards, the messy drawers at home where all the knick-knacks go, and kept my eyes open for trinkets at flea markets.

Arrow shaped post-its. Not all stationary shops carry these. If you do an internet search for 'arrow-shaped post-its', you will find either stationary or training shops that do. Amazon usually does too.

Wooden figures. The figures are easiest to find when you search for 'wooden figures to paint'. Amazon carries different ones and they can often also be found in hobby stores.

Acknowledgements

The impulse for this book came as a surprise. I had played around with the idea of writing years ago yet had never even put a word down and consequently buried the idea. Until, while teaching, someone asked, 'Where can I read more about working and coaching with the right brain?'. And the proverbial lightbulb went off in my head; this is my book to write.

Between then and now, many people have been guides, helpers and supporters on this journey. I am grateful for their generosity and thank them all from the bottom of my heart.

The book is dedicated to my family; they are my roots, source of inspiration and energy, and have supported this work in many ways. Our daughter Julie, student of biosciences, has done most of the drawings, artfully translating my scribbles into wonderful illustrations. Our daughter Charlotte, a talented writer, scrutinized the final versions with her eye for detail and language, and taught me how to do references. Laurent, my love and husband, pushed the logic and coherence to a whole new level, with his never-failing humor and persistence. Joeke, my mother with her ample right brain wisdom, offered valuable advice and words of encouragement exactly when I needed it. A special word for my father Kees, who, a few weeks before he passed away, read the introduction. With his remarkable ability to focus on what truly matters, he redirected the tone of the book.

My knowledgeable colleague Mike Barkham rigorously tested the first draft and helped to fine-tune the content. Experienced leaders and long-time friends, Allard Creyghton and Mirko Nicolic, provided direction and validation from a leadership perspective. Rebecca Rumsey, Peter Melrose, Sarah LeRoy and Andrew Rumsey gave thoughtful comments on different drafts. Rosa Williams, gifted young artist, made several of the book's illustrations, including the beautiful hands and Stuart Brett added his experienced eye and skills to finalize the cover.

My editor, Lissa Gibbins, helped me through this writing process with excellent practical advice as well as her gift to make words flow. As a non-native English speaker, I was rather worried that my writing was too simplistic. Even when it was, Lissa never showed it yet gracefully adjusted where needed. In the early days, writer Colin Heber-Percy, reviewed the book outline and suggested what is now the title of the book – what a gift that was. Jay Thompson from UK book publishing provided the finishing touch to prepare the book and patiently helped to resolve all the last hurdles.

When Katja Bossert started the BA coaching academy, a quality program that would soon receive top ICF accreditation, she asked me to teach what coaches need to know about the brain. I immediately agreed thinking I was doing a favor for a good friend. How the tables have turned! Not only has the teaching been an absolute pleasure, it has also been intellectually stimulating and, ultimately, has lead to this book. My thanks Katja, for your unwavering belief in what we can do together.

And finally, my deep gratitude to my coachees whose conversations inspired all the examples in this book. They shall remain anonymous, but you know who you are as you each approved the use of our work. In a few cases, I could not reach the person that inspired an example; those examples have been further adjusted to protect confidentiality. Thank you so much for the privilege of working together and for allowing me to share pieces of our conversations in this book.

My scientific understanding of the brain has been informed by the work, research and writings of many remarkable scientists and academics. Details can be found in the references. There are three people whose work I would especially like to highlight. In 'Mindsight, Daniel Siegel shares an integrated view on how we function based on his years of practice as a therapist, complimented with a relentless intellectual curiosity across scientific fields. The stories of his work with clients are unique, touching and insightful. They captured my interest at the start of my coaching career and segmented my focus on finding practical applications in coaching and leadership development for insights from the fields of neuroscience and neurobiology. I first came across Jill Bolte-Taylor's 'My Stroke of Insight' on the TED platform. Hearing her tell the story of her right-brain experience was a pivotal moment in my coaching and teaching practice. It gave words to what I had been practicing for years yet never been able to articulate, the experience of 'we'. Finally, Iain McGilchrist's extraordinary work, 'The Master and his Emissary', provided the majority of the scientific underpinning for the ideas in this book. I am deeply conscious that my simplifications in no way do justice to the depth of McGilchrist's work and, for anyone keen to truly understand the left and the right side of the brain, his book is a must-read.

To Iain McGilchrist, Jill Bolte Taylor and Dan Siegel, my sincere thanks for your meaningful works that have provided me with years of inspiration.

References

1. The BA coaching academy, Munich, Germany offers coaching training programs at different levels, with accrecitation by the ICF (International Coach Federation). For more information, see https://www.bossert-associates.com/coaching-academy

2. Siegel, D.J. (2011). *Mindsight: the New Science of Personal Transformation*. New York: Bantam Books, pp.108–109

3. Corballis, M.C. (2014). Left Brain, Right Brain: Facts and Fantasies. *PLoS Biology*, 12(1). Available at: https://www.ncbi.nlm.nih.gov

4. Bolte Taylor, J. (2011). *My Stroke of Insight A Brain Scientist's Personal Journey*. London Hodder & Stoughton General Division, p.29-31

5. McGilchrist, I. (2019). *The Master And His Emissary: the divided brain and the making of the western world*. New Expanded paperback ed. Yale University Press, pp.3

6. Bolte Taylor, J. (2008). *My stroke of insight. TED.* Available at: https://www.ted.com

7. Bolte Taylor, 2011, p.30

8. Perls, F.S., Hefferline, R.F. and Goodman, P. (2013). *Gestalt Therapy: Excitement and Growth in the Human Personality.* London Souvenir Press. First published in 1951

9. McGilchrist, 2018, p.40

10. Downey, M. (2003). *Effective coaching: lessons from the coaches' coach.* New York; London: Texere, p.21

11. Siegel, 2011, p.107

12. Dutton, D.G. and Aron, A.P. (1974). Some evidence for heightened sexual attraction under conditions of high anxiety. *Journal of Personality and Social Psychology,* 30(4), pp.510–517

13. Cattaneo, L. and Rizzolatti, G. (2009). The Mirror Neuron System. *Archives of Neurology,* 66(5)

14. ten Brinke, L. and Weisbuch, M. (2020). How verbal-nonverbal consistency shapes the truth. *Journal of Experimental Social Psychology,* 89, p.103978

15. Tversky, B. (2019). *Mind in Motion: How Action Shapes Thought.* Basic Civitas Books

16. Center for Creative Leadership, Visual ExplorerTM Special Edition

17. Center for Creative Leadership, Visual ExplorerTM

18. Center for Creative Leadership, Visual ExplorerTM, copyright Getty Images

19. Center for Creative Leadership, Visual ExplorerTM, copyright Getty Images

20. Achor, S. (2011). *The happiness advantage: the seven principles that fuel success and performance at work.* London: Virgin, p.100

21. *The Wolf of Wallstreet.* (2013). [Film] Paramount pictures. Jordan Belfort (book), Terrence Winter (screenplay)

22. Derived from Grant, A.M. (2012). ROI is a poor measure of coaching success: towards a more holistic approach using a well-being and engagement framework. *Coaching: An International Journal of Theory, Research and Practice,* 5(2), pp.74–85

23. Rock, D. (2009). *Your Brain at Work, strategies for overcoming distraction, regaining focus and working smarter all day long.* New York Harper Collins. p.105

24. Diziker, P. (2015). The Many Careers of Jay Forrester. *MIT Technology review.* Available at: https://www.technologyreview.com

25. https://mitsloan.mit.edu/faculty/academic-groups/system-dynamics/about-us

26. Kerr, M.E. and Bowen, M. (1988). *Family evaluation: An approach based on Bowen theory.* New York: Norton

27. Manné, J. (2009). *Family constellations: a practical guide to uncovering the origins of family conflict.* Berkeley, Calif.: North Atlantic Books

28. Whittington, J. (2016). *Systemic coaching and constellations: the principles, practices and application for individuals, teams and groups.* London: Kogan Page

29. Clark, J.M. and Paivio, A. (1991). Dual coding theory and education. *Educational Psychology Review,* 3(3), pp.149–210

30. Siegel, 2011, pp. 108-109

31. Collings English Dictionary

32. Profit & Loss

33. Siegel, 2011. P.107

34. Headspace. (2020). *Meditation and Sleep Made Simple - Headspace.* Available at: https://Headspace.com

35. Clark, A. (2013). Whatever next? Predictive brains, situated agents, and the future of cognitive science. *Behavioral and Brain sciences, 36,* pp.181–204

36. Klein, G.A. (2017). *Sources of power: how people make decisions.* Cambridge, Ma: MIT Press, p.34

37. Gilbert, D. (2014). 'The psychology of your future self. TED. Available at: https://www.ted.com

38. Cuddy, A. (2012). *Your body language may shape who you are. TED.* Available at: https://www.ted.com

39. Cuddy, A. (2018). *Presence: bringing your boldest self to your biggest challenges.* New York: Back Bay Books, ©Bb

40. Schmittlein, D. (May 3, 2021) at on-line event "An experience made to matter" in a discussion on the future of management education

41. Koontz, K. (2018). Listening in with Jill Bolte Taylor. *Unity magazine.* Available at: https://www.unity.org

42. Kimmel, M. (2015). *Why gender equality is good for everyone — men included. TED.* Available at: https://www.ted.com

43. Project Implicit (2013). *Project Implicit.* Harvard.edu. Available at: https://implicit.harvard.edu

44. Gino, F. and Coffman, K. (2021). Unconscious Bias Training that Works. *Harvard Business Review,* September – October, 2021

45. Cuddy, 2018

46. Kinsey Goman, C. (2011). *The silent language of leaders: How body language can help or hurt how you lead.* San Francisco, Calif.: Jossey-Bass

47. Willis, J. and Todorov, A. (2006). First impressions: Making up your mind after a 100-ms exposure to a face. *Psychological Science,* 17(7), pp.592–598

48. Sorenson, S. (2013). How employee engagement drives growth. *Gallup Business Journal*. Available at: https://www.gallup.com/workplace

49. De Smet et al., A. (2021). 'Great Attrition' or 'Great Attraction", the choice is yours. *McKinsey Quarterly*. Available at: https://www.mckinsey.com

50. Harter, J. (2022). U.S. Employee Engagement Drops for First Year in a Decade. *Workplace*. Available at: https://www.gallup.com/workplace